EASY
KEYBOARD
SONGS FOR BEGINNERS

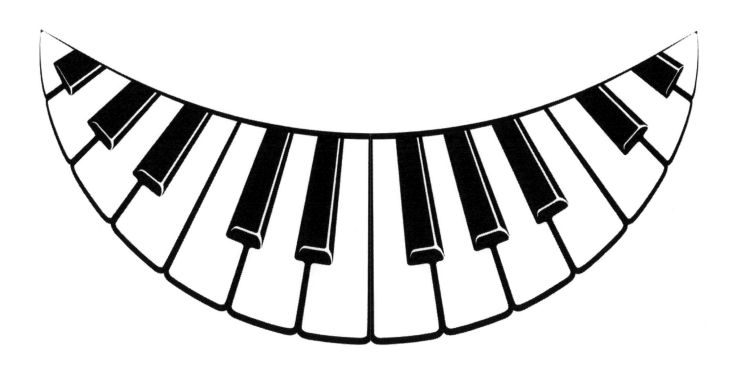

www.EasySongbooks.com

Contents

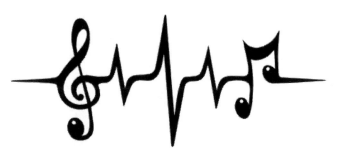

Mary Had a Little Lamb

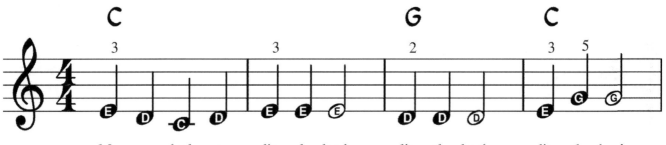

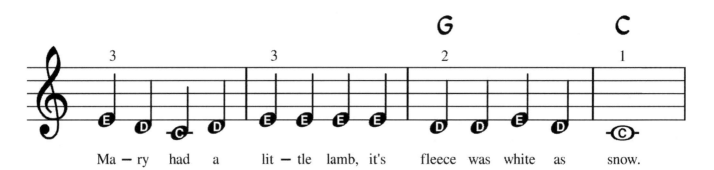

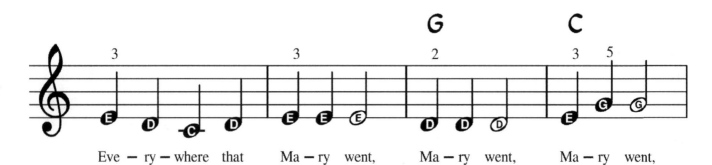

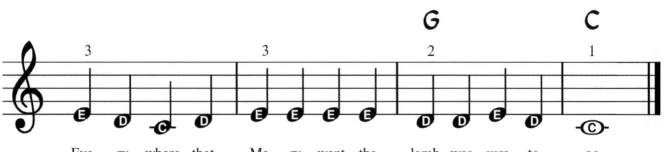

Twinkle Twinkle Little Star

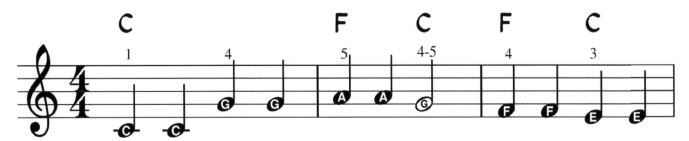

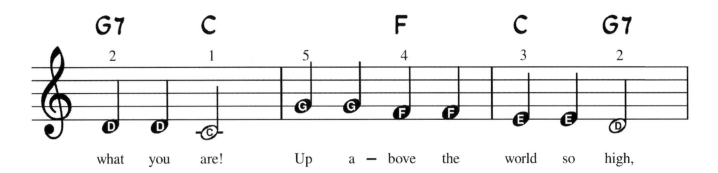

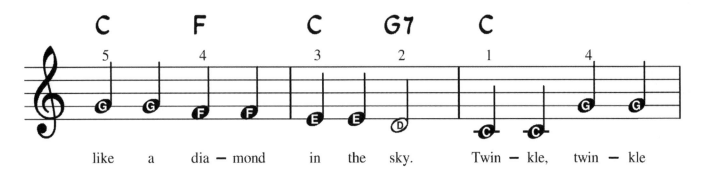

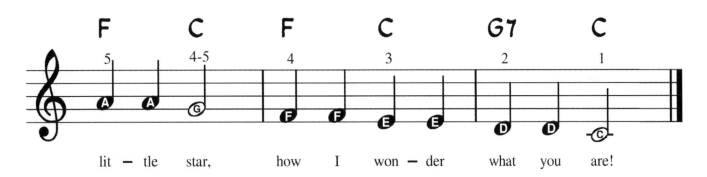

Can Can

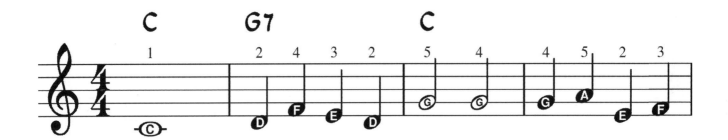

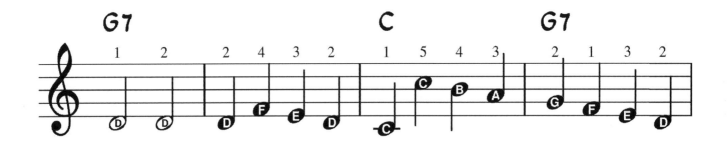

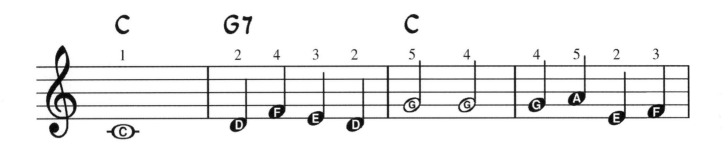

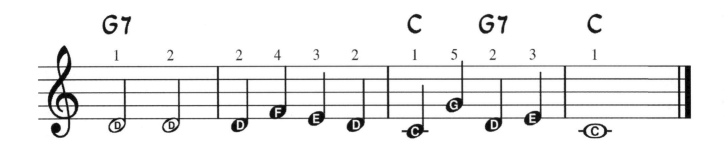

Baa, Baa, Black Sheep

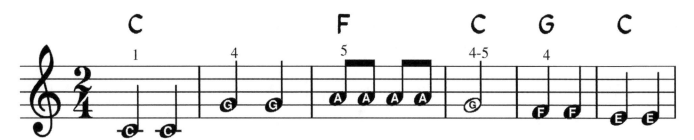

Baa, baa, black sheep, have you a – ny wool? Yes sir, yes sir,

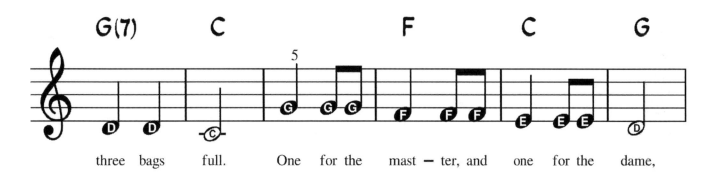

three bags full. One for the mast – ter, and one for the dame,

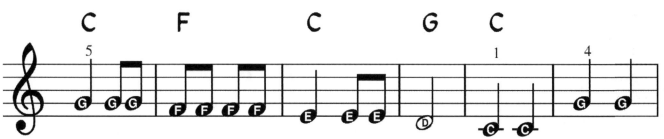

one for the lit – tle boy who lives down the lane. Baa, baa, black sheep,

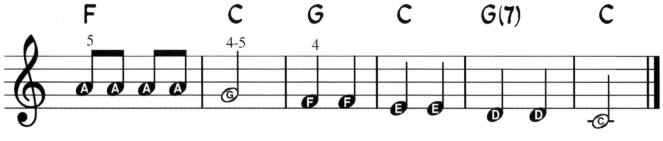

have you a – ny wool? Yes sir, yes sir, three bags full.

Ode To Joy

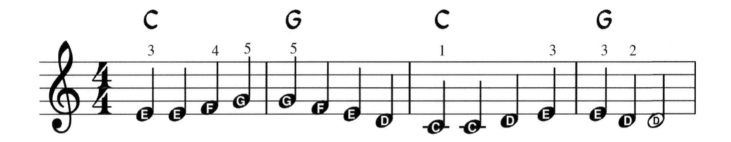

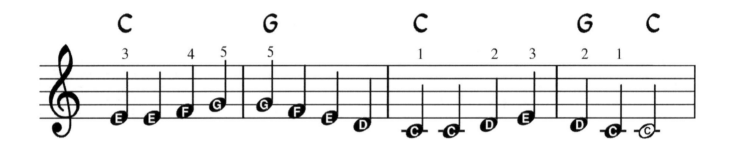

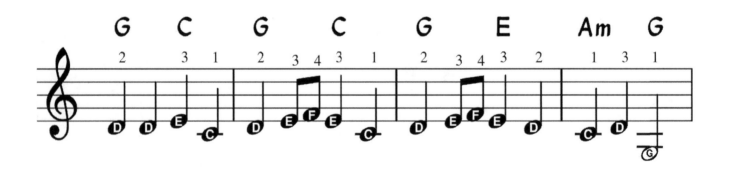

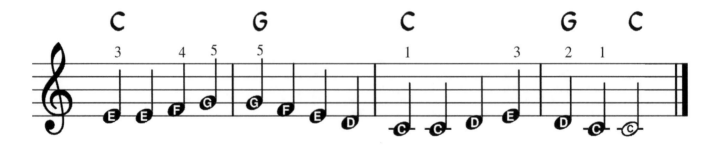

Skip To My Lou

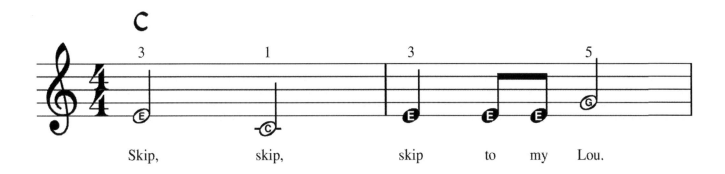

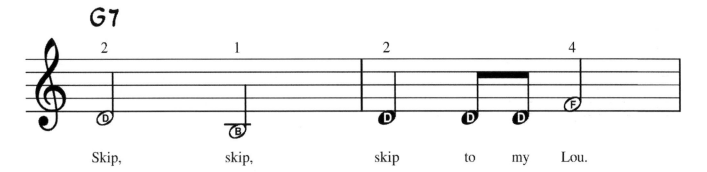

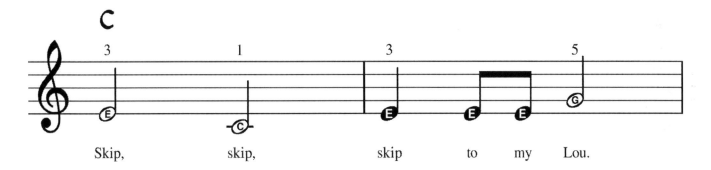

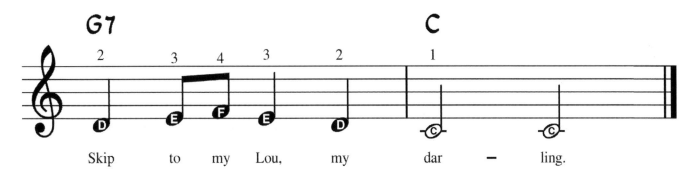

Drink To Me Only With Thine Eyes

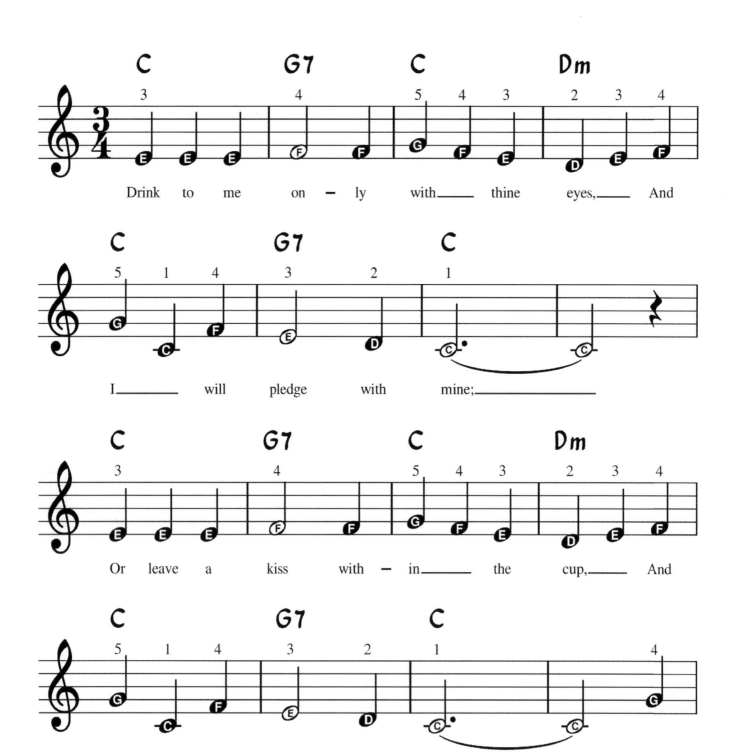

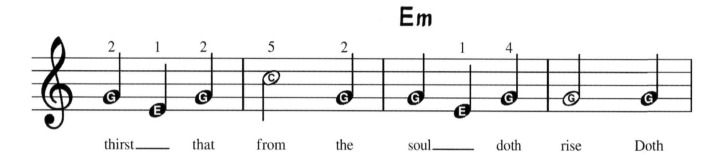

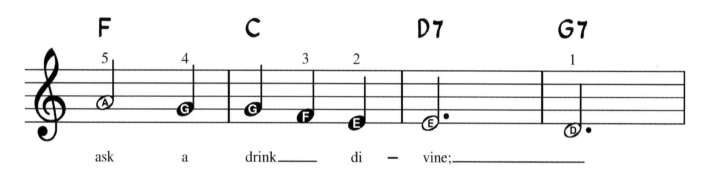

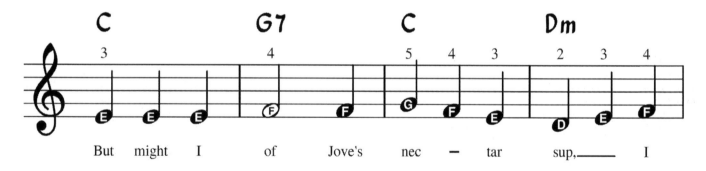

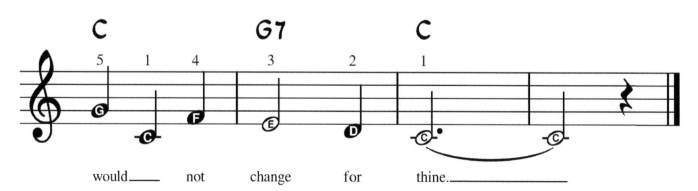

11

This Old Man

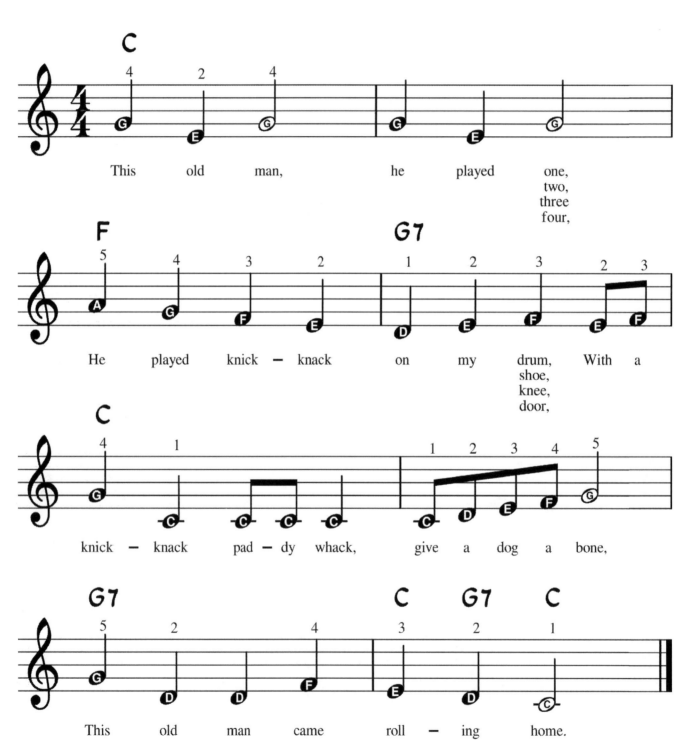

Row, Row, Row Your Boat

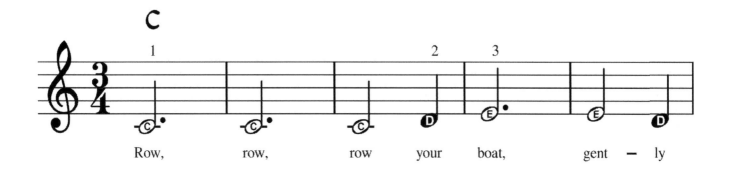

Row, row, row your boat, gent — ly

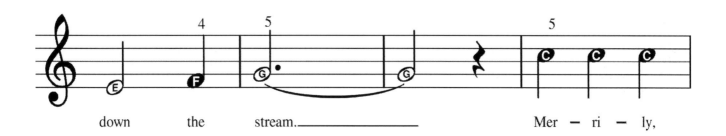

down the stream._____ Mer — ri — ly,

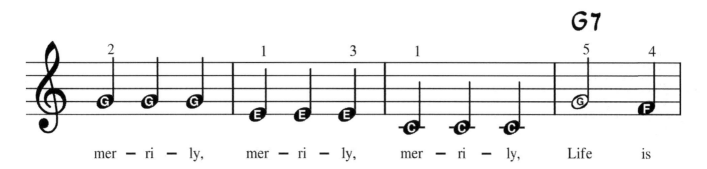

mer — ri — ly, mer — ri — ly, mer — ri — ly, Life is

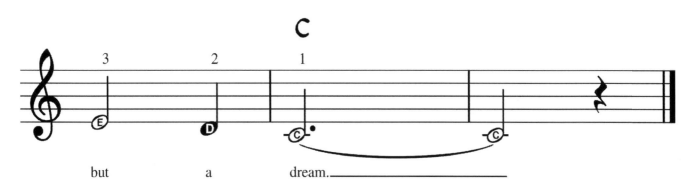

but a dream._____

Three Blind Mice

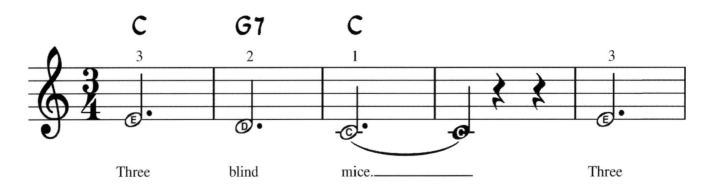

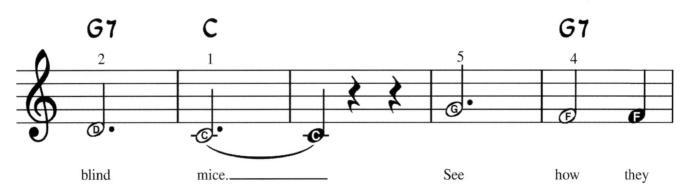

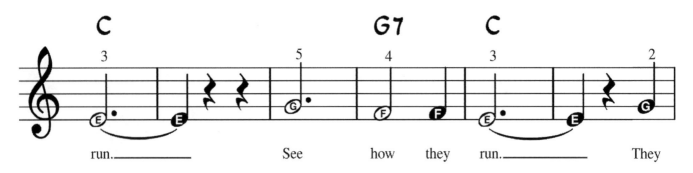

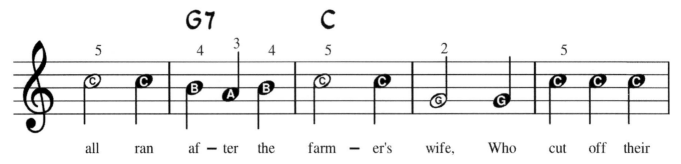

G7 — **C** — **G7**

tails with a carv — ing knife, Did you ev — er see such a

C — **G7** — **C**

sight in your life, As three blind mice?_____

When The Saints Go Marching In

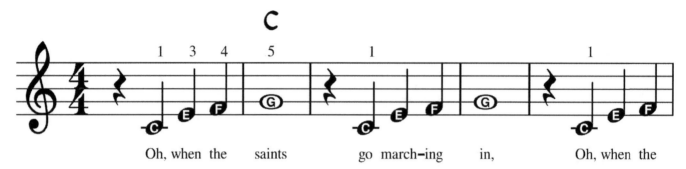

Oh, when the saints go march-ing in, Oh, when the

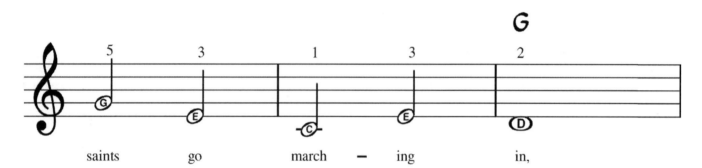

saints go march — ing in,

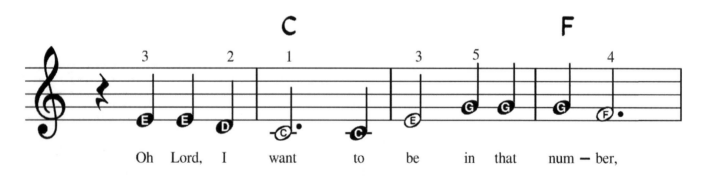

Oh Lord, I want to be in that num — ber,

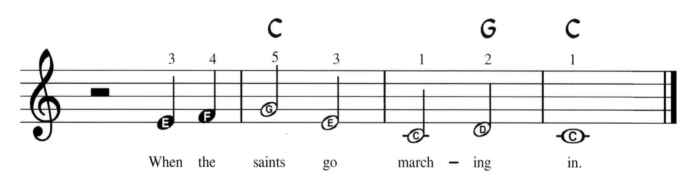

When the saints go march — ing in.

The Grand Old Duke Of York

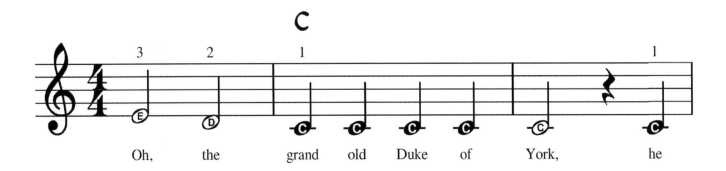

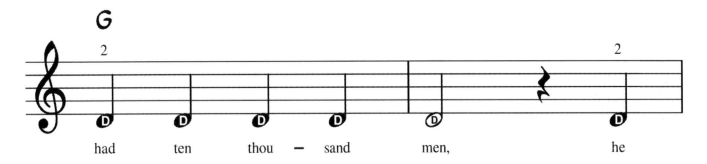

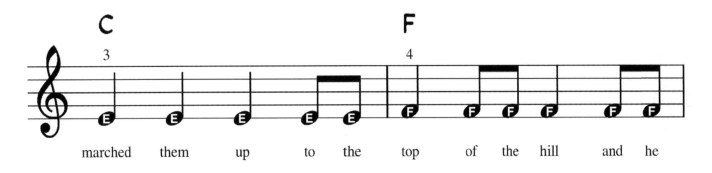

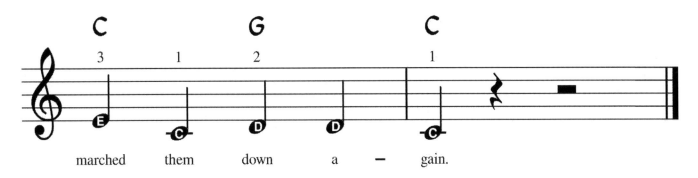

The Muffin Man

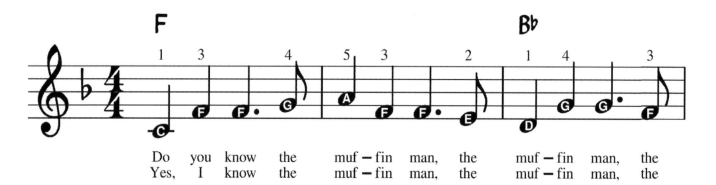

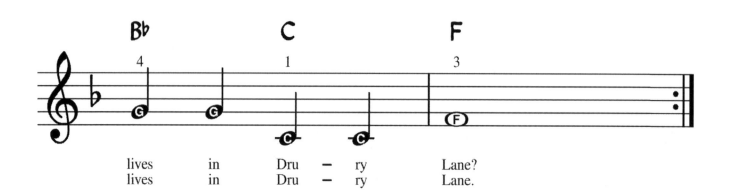

Lavender's Blue

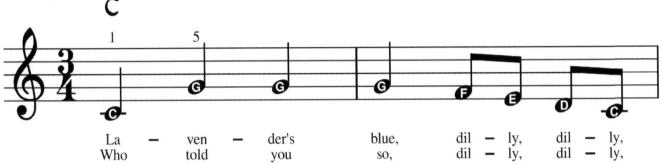

La — ven — der's blue, dil — ly, dil — ly,
Who told you so, dil — ly, dil — ly,

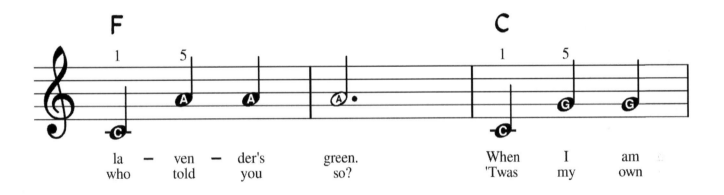

la — ven — der's green. When I am
who told you so? 'Twas my own

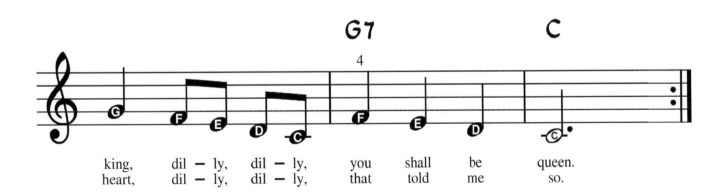

king, dil — ly, dil — ly, you shall be queen.
heart, dil — ly, dil — ly, that told me so.

Jingle Bells

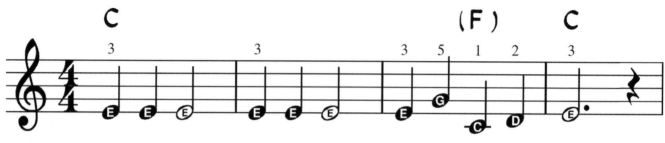

Jin — gle bells, jin — gle bells, jin — gle all the way.

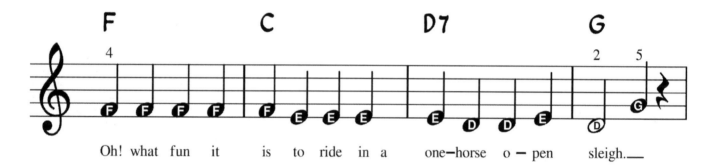

Oh! what fun it is to ride in a one—horse o — pen sleigh.___

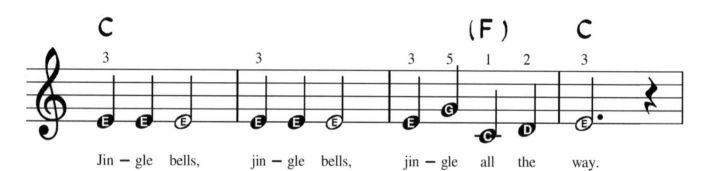

Jin — gle bells, jin — gle bells, jin — gle all the way.

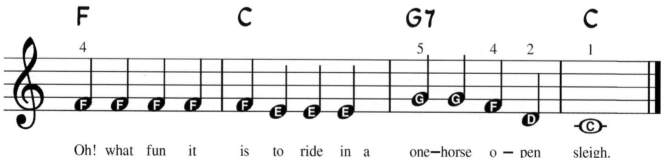

Oh! what fun it is to ride in a one—horse o — pen sleigh.

Kum Ba Yah

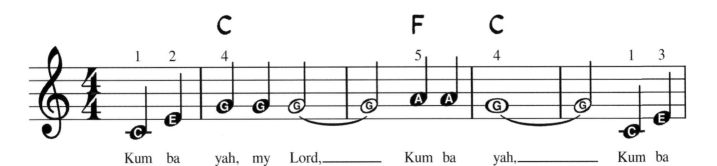

Kum ba yah, my Lord,_____ Kum ba yah,_____ Kum ba

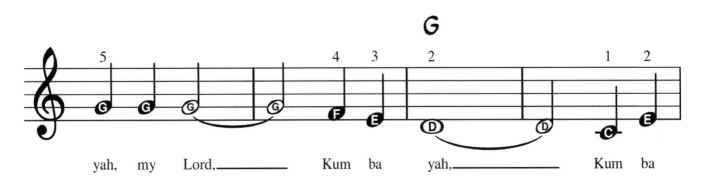

yah, my Lord,_____ Kum ba yah,_____ Kum ba

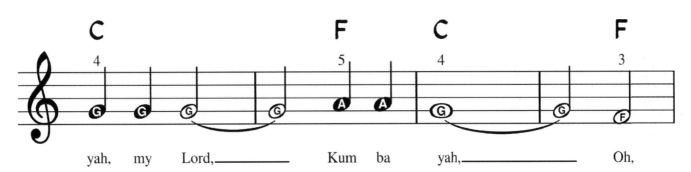

yah, my Lord,_____ Kum ba yah,_____ Oh,

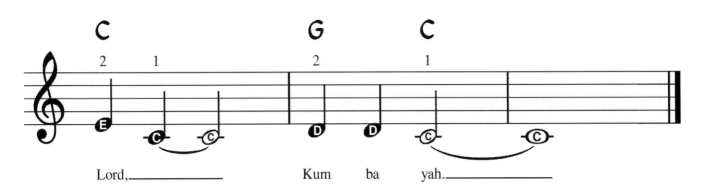

Lord,_____ Kum ba yah._____

Alphabet Song

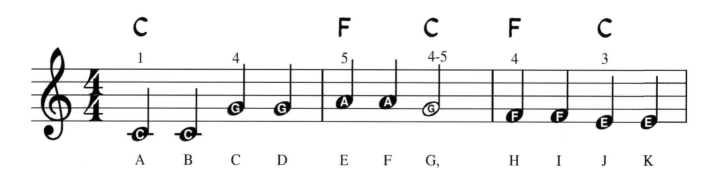

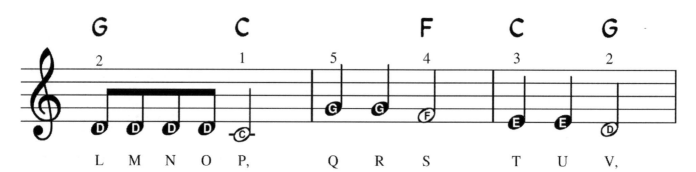

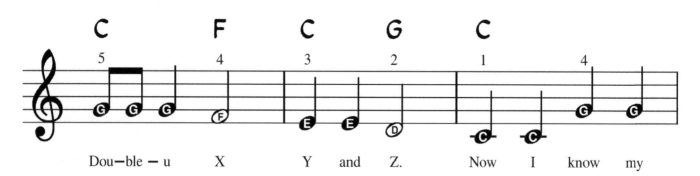

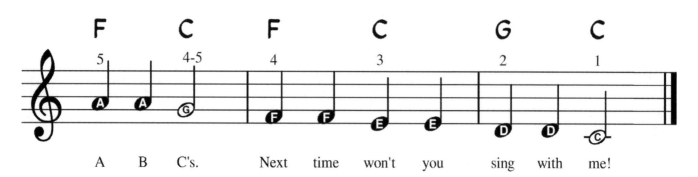

Oh! Susanna

I_____ come from A — la — ba — ma with my ban—jo on my

knee. I'm_____ goin' to Loui — si — a — na, my_____ true love for to

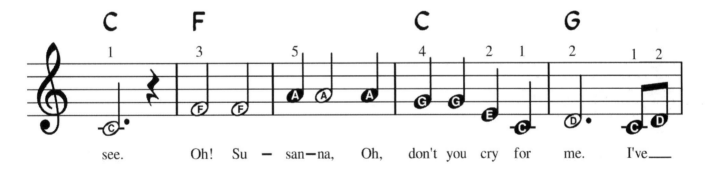

see. Oh! Su — san—na, Oh, don't you cry for me. I've_____

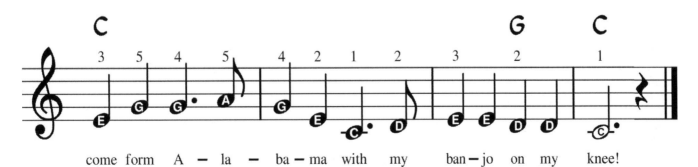

come form A — la — ba—ma with my ban—jo on my knee!

London Bridge

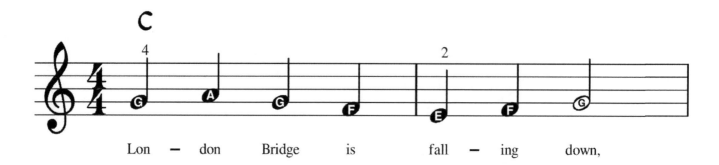

Lon — don Bridge is fall — ing down,

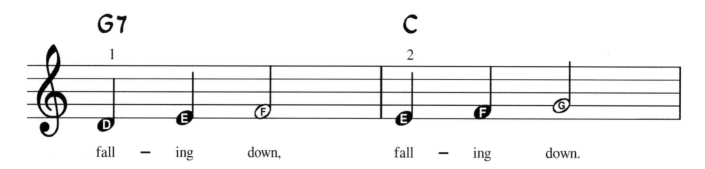

fall — ing down, fall — ing down.

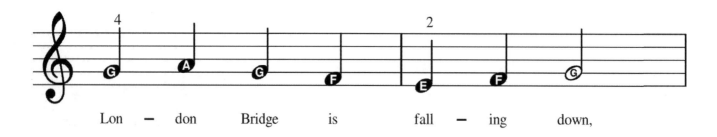

Lon — don Bridge is fall — ing down,

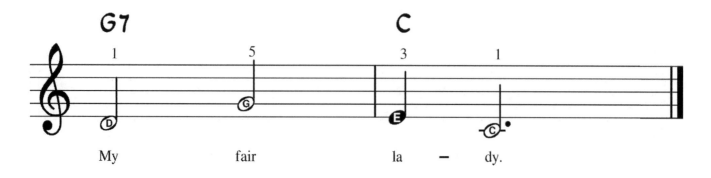

My fair la — dy.

Old MacDonald

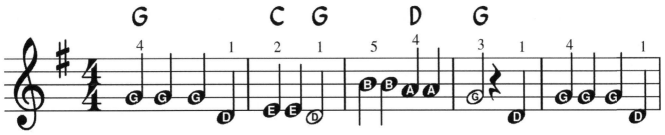

Old Mac-Don-ald   had a farm,   E – I – E – I – O.   And   on this farm he

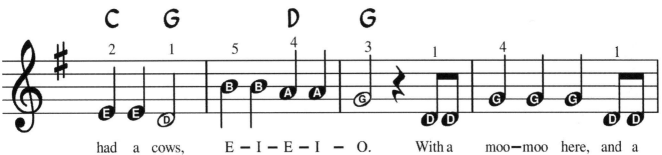

had a cows,   E – I – E – I – O.   With a   moo–moo here, and a

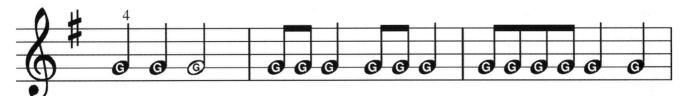

moo–moo there,   Here–a moo, there–a moo,   Eve–ry where a moo   moo.

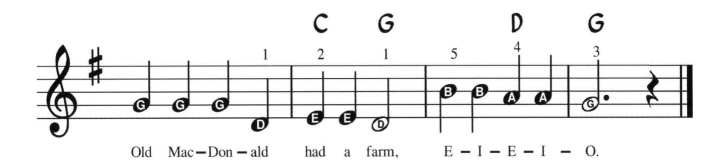

Old Mac–Don–ald   had a farm,   E – I – E – I – O.

Are You Sleeping?

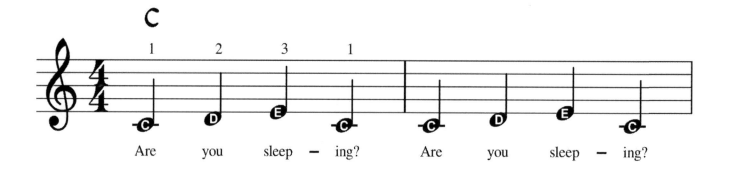

Are you sleep — ing? Are you sleep — ing?

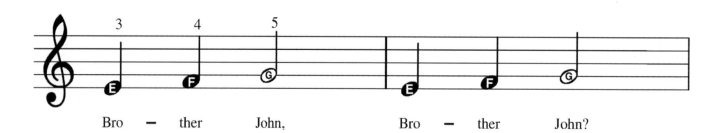

Bro — ther John, Bro — ther John?

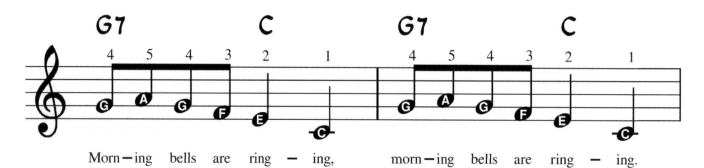

Morn—ing bells are ring — ing, morn—ing bells are ring — ing.

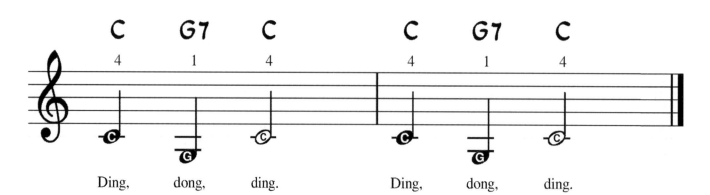

Ding, dong, ding. Ding, dong, ding.

Brahms' Lullaby

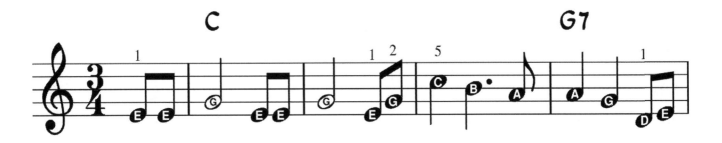

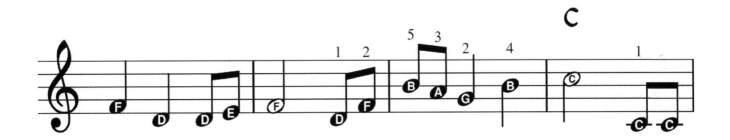

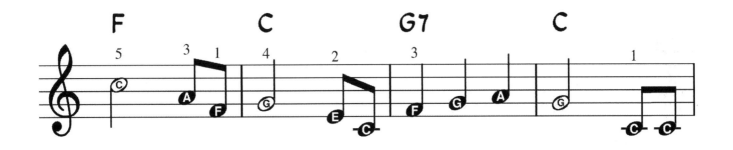

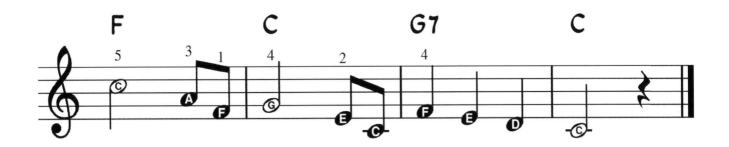

Amazing Grace

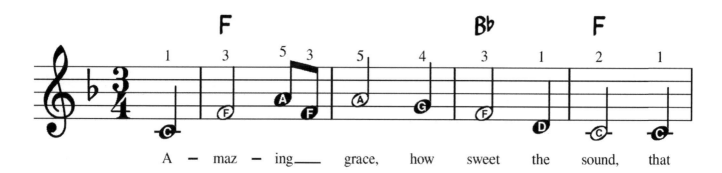

A – maz – ing___ grace, how sweet the sound, that

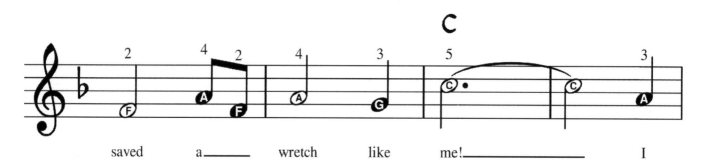

saved a___ wretch like me!___ I

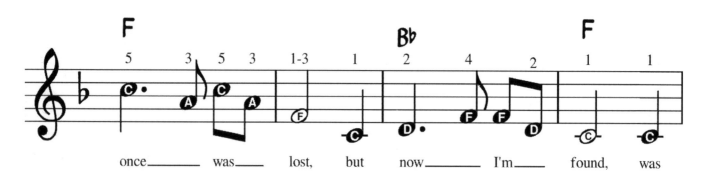

once___ was___ lost, but now___ I'm___ found, was

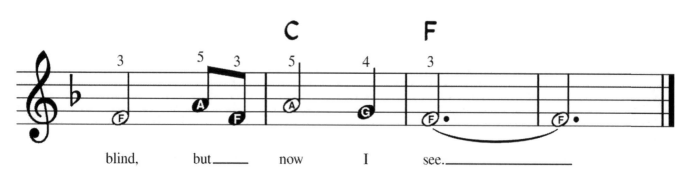

blind, but___ now I see.___

Clementine (Oh, My Darling)

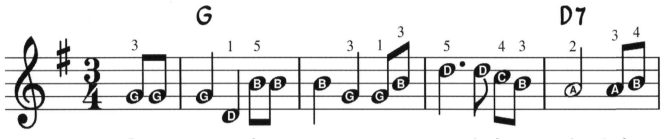

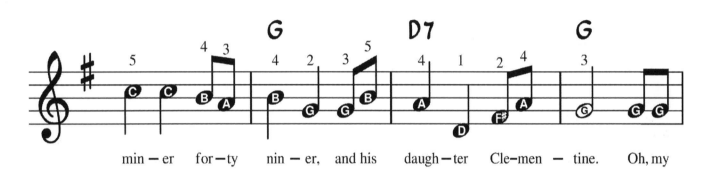

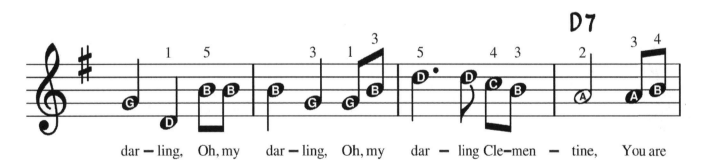

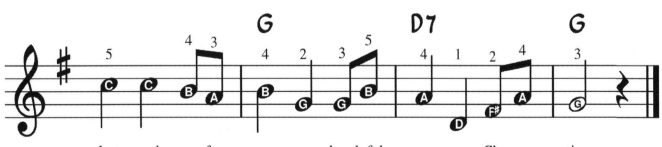

A-Tisket, A-Tasket

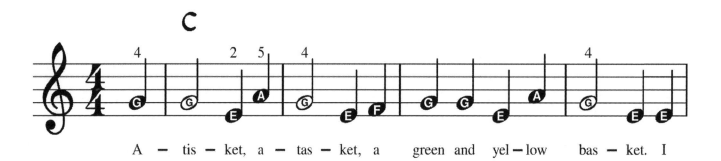

A — tis — ket, a — tas — ket, a   green and yel — low   bas — ket. I

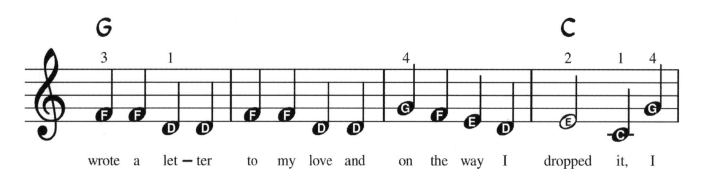

wrote a let — ter   to my love and   on the way I   dropped it, I

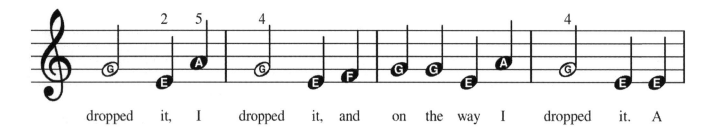

dropped it,   I   dropped it,   and   on the way I   dropped it.   A

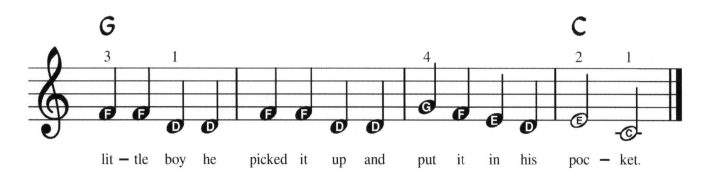

lit — tle boy he   picked it   up and   put it in his   poc — ket.

Drunken Sailor

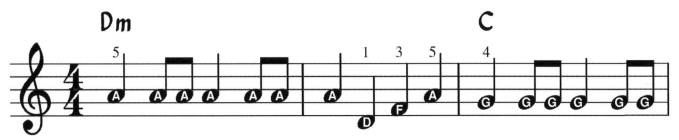

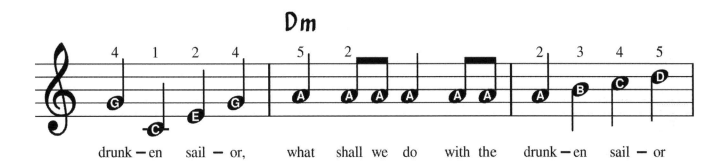

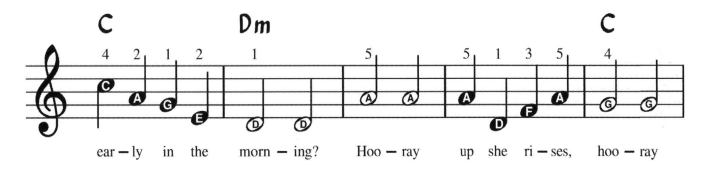

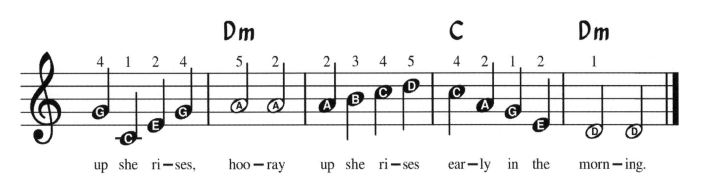

Girls and Boys

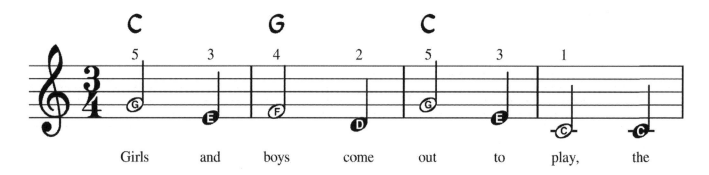

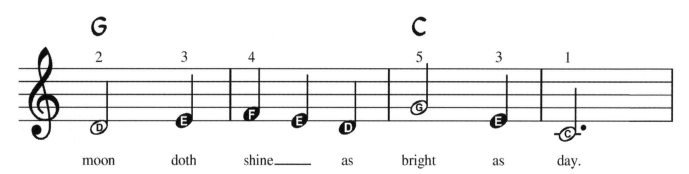

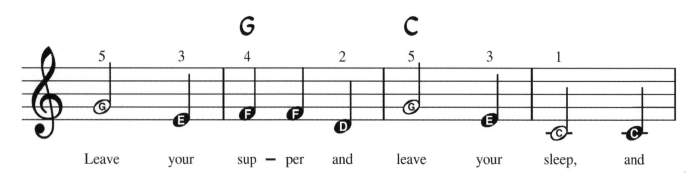

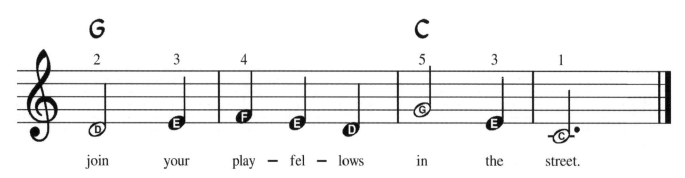

Happy Birthday

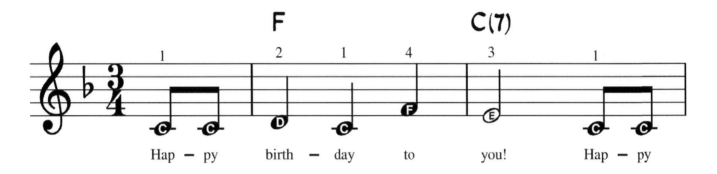

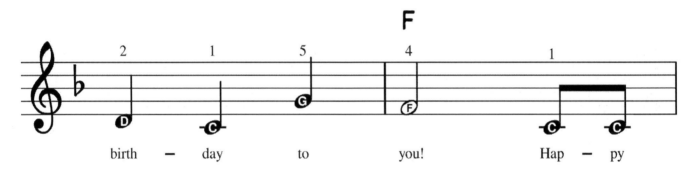

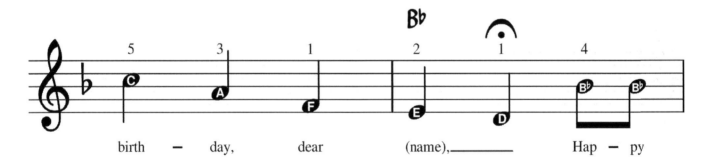

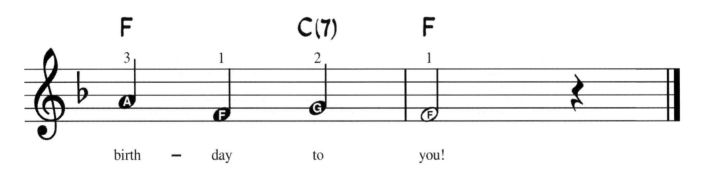

33

Hickory Dickory Dock

Humpty Dumpty

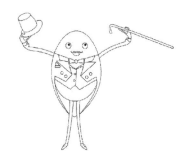
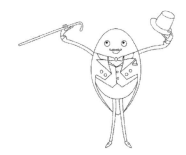

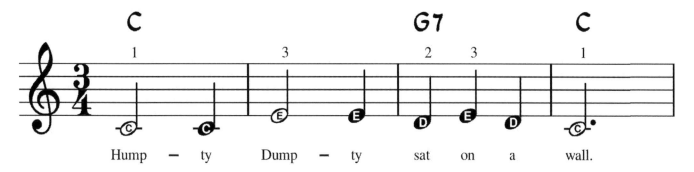

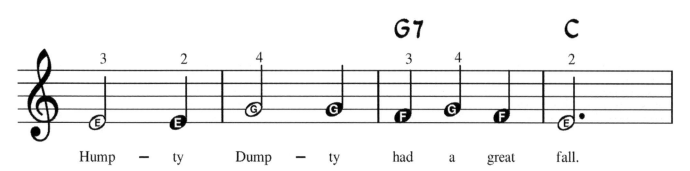

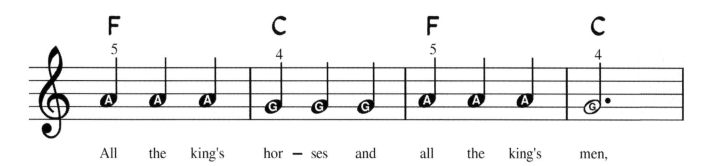

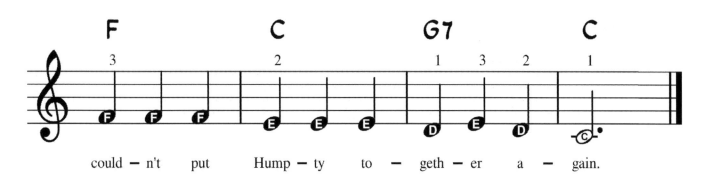

My Bonnie Lies Over The Ocean

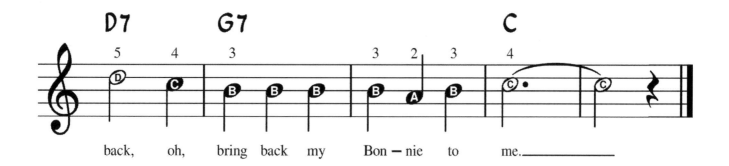

back, oh, bring back my Bon — nie to me._____

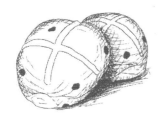

Hot Cross Buns

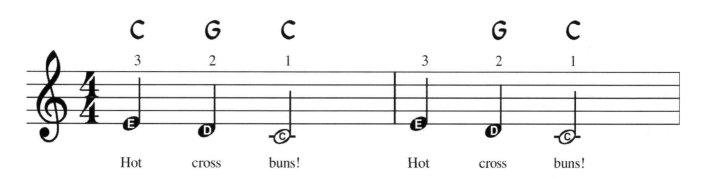

Hot cross buns! Hot cross buns!

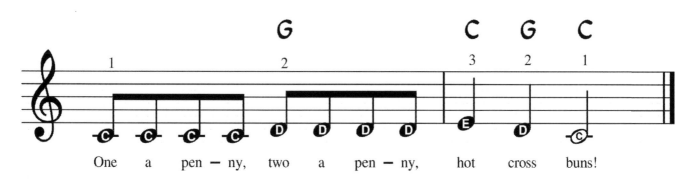

One a pen — ny, two a pen — ny, hot cross buns!

Polly Put The Kettle On

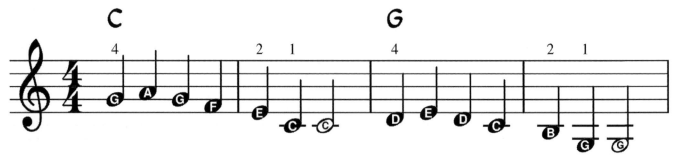

Pol — ly, put the ket — tle on, Pol — ly, put the ket — tle on,

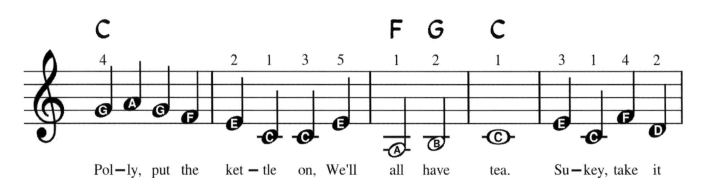

Pol — ly, put the ket — tle on, We'll all have tea. Su — key, take it

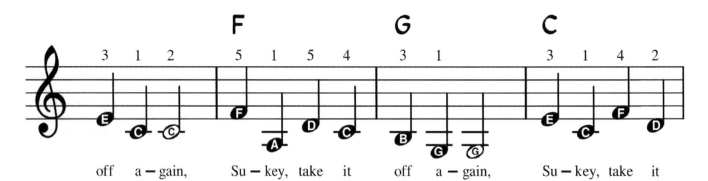

off a — gain, Su — key, take it off a — gain, Su — key, take it

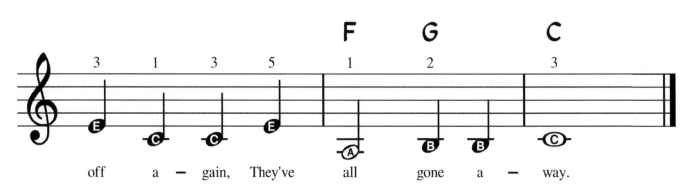

off a — gain, They've all gone a — way.

Pop! Goes the Weasel

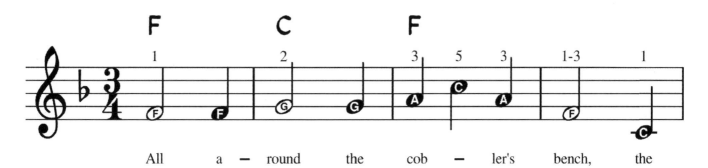

All a — round the cob — ler's bench, the

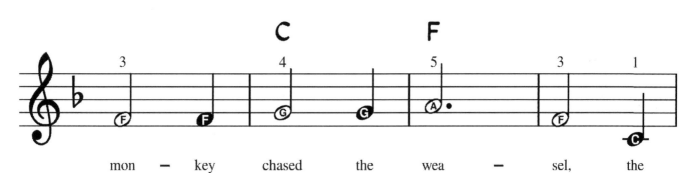

mon — key chased the wea — sel, the

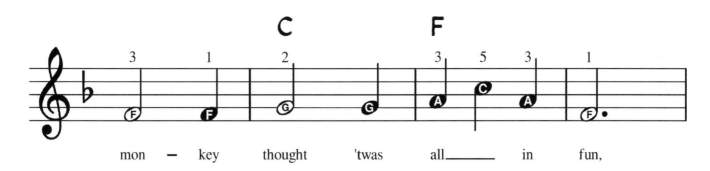

mon — key thought 'twas all_____ in fun,

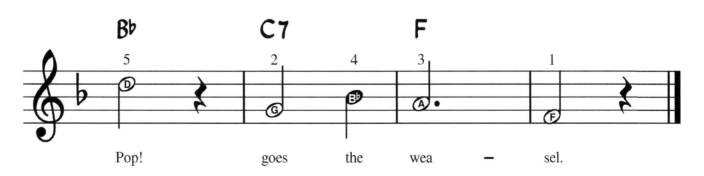

Pop! goes the wea — sel.

Rock-A-Bye, Baby

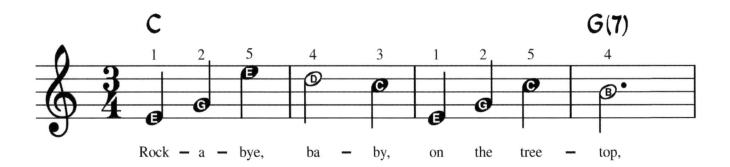

Rock — a — bye,   ba — by,   on   the   tree — top,

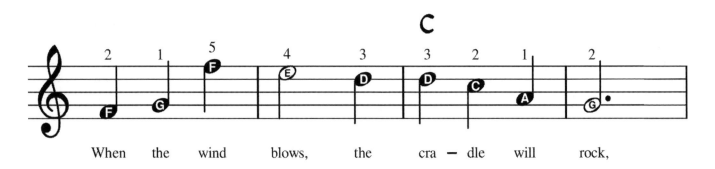

When   the   wind   blows,   the   cra — dle   will   rock,

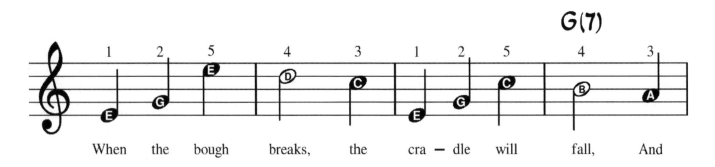

When   the   bough   breaks,   the   cra — dle   will   fall,   And

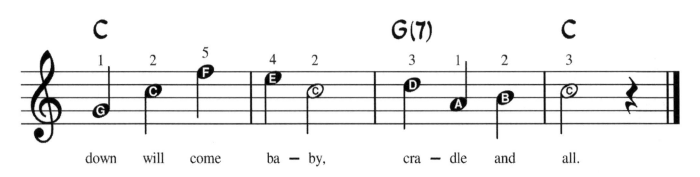

down   will   come   ba — by,   cra — dle   and   all.

Scarborough Fair

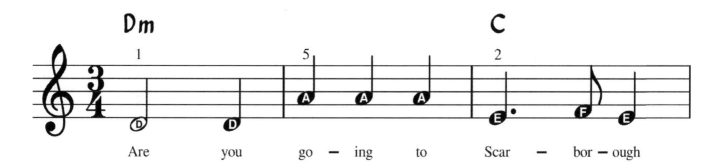

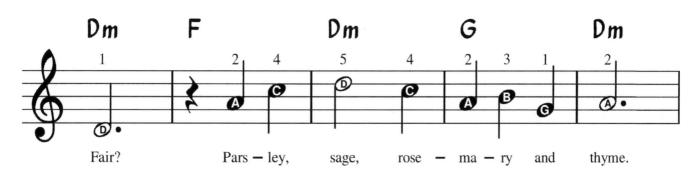

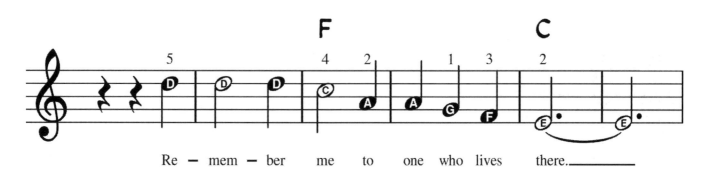

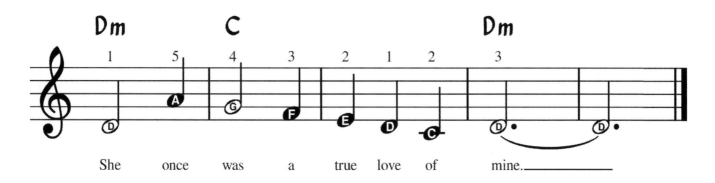

Silent Night

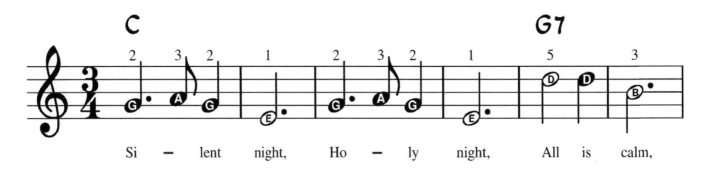

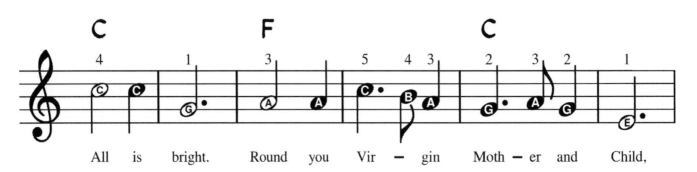

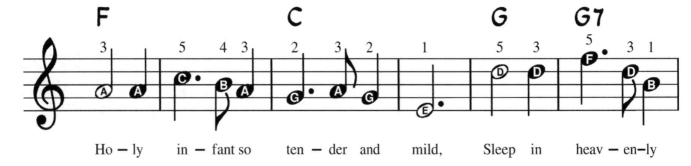

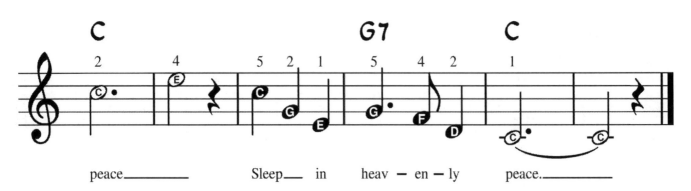

Oranges And Lemons

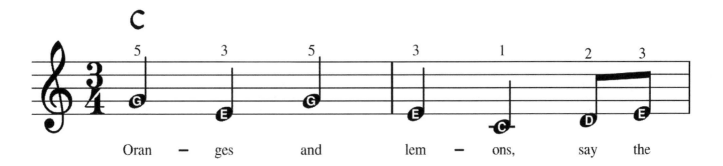

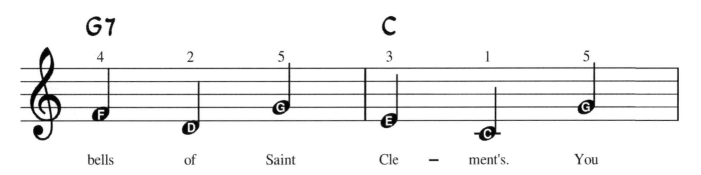

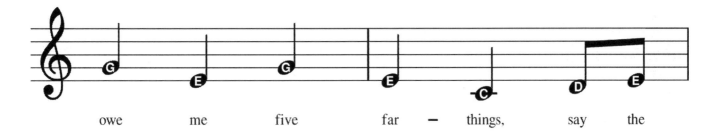

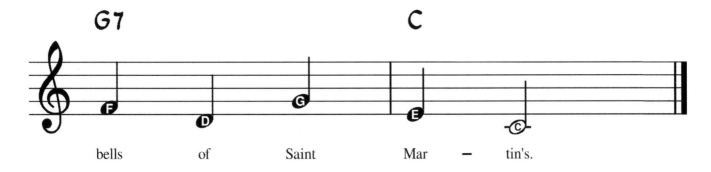

Ring a Ring o' Roses

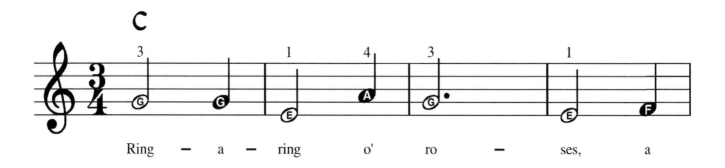

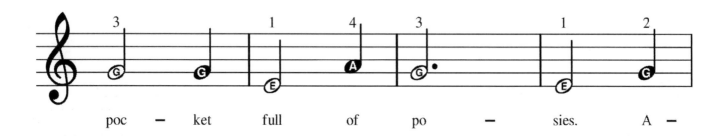

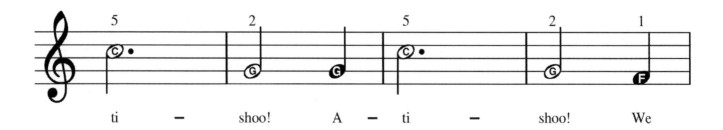

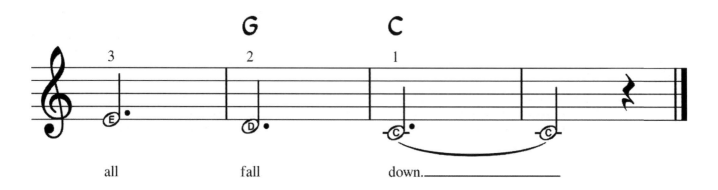

Hush, Little Baby

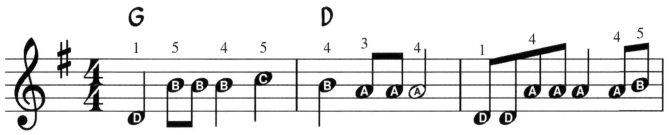

Hush,	lit—tle	ba — by,	don't	say	a	word,	Pa–pa's	gon—na	buy	you	a
If	that	dia—mond	ring	turns	brass,	Pa–pa's	gon—na	buy	you	a
If	that	bil — ly	goat	won't	pull,	Pa–pa's	gon—na	buy	you	a
If	that	dog named	Rover	won't	bark,	Pa–pa's	gon—na	buy	you	a

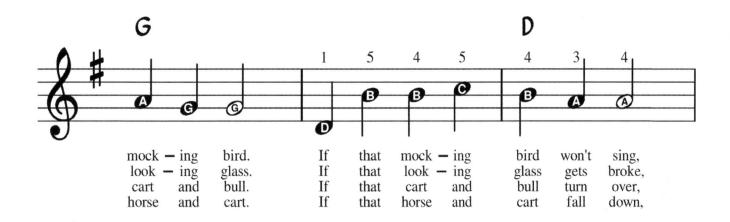

mock — ing	bird.	If	that	mock — ing	bird	won't	sing,
look — ing	glass.	If	that	look — ing	glass	gets	broke,
cart	and	bull.	If	that	cart	and	bull	turn	over,
horse	and	cart.	If	that	horse	and	cart	fall	down,

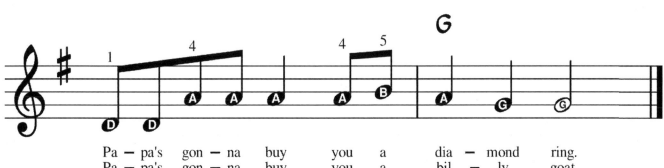

Pa — pa's	gon — na	buy	you	a	dia — mond	ring.
Pa — pa's	gon — na	buy	you	a	bil — ly	goat.
Pa — pa's	gon — na	buy	you	a	dog	named	Rover.
You'll	still	be	the	sweetest	lit — tle	baby	in	town.

All Things Bright And Beautiful

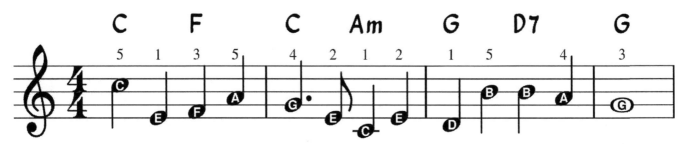

All things bright and beau—ti—ful, All crea—tures great and small,

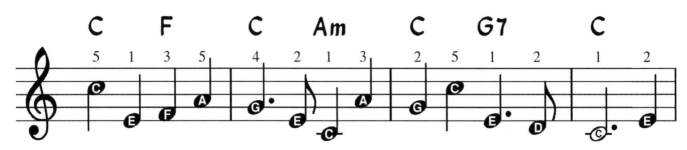

All things wise and won—der—ful: The Lord God made them all. Each

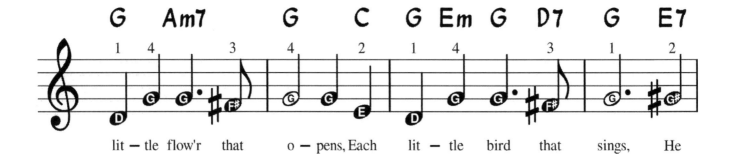

lit—tle flow'r that o—pens, Each lit—tle bird that sings, He

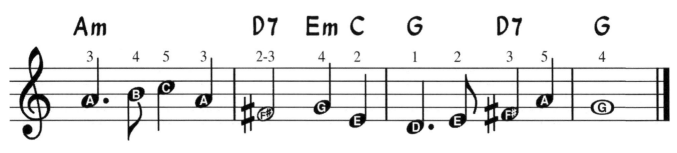

made their glow—ing col—ors, He made their ti—ny wings.

46

Jack and Jill

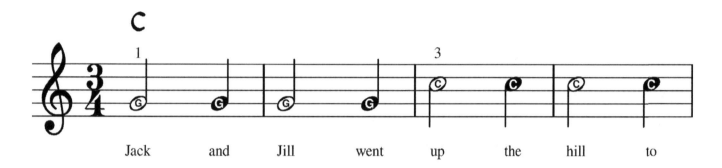

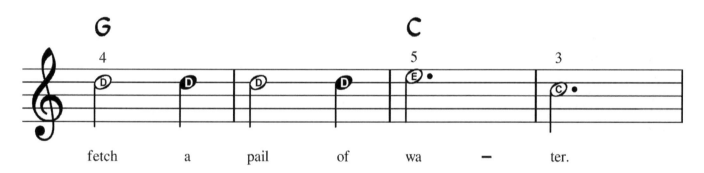

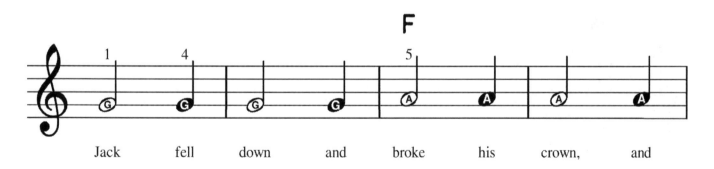

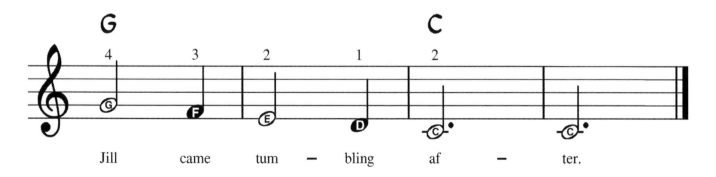

47

Au Clair De La Lune

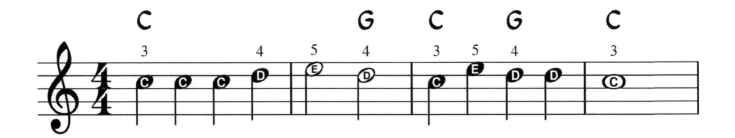

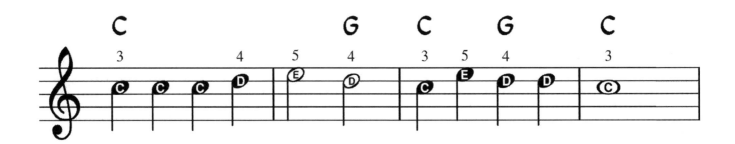

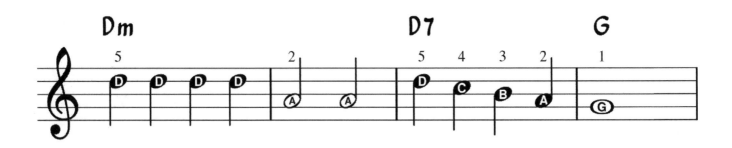

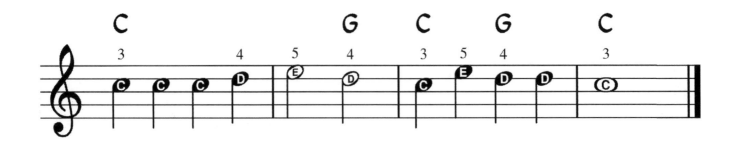

Hey, Diddle Diddle

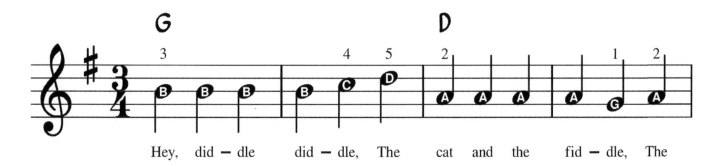

Hey, did — dle did — dle, The cat and the fid — dle, The

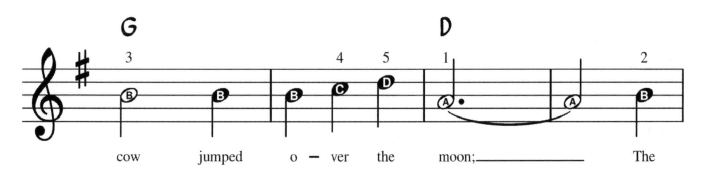

cow jumped o — ver the moon;_____ The

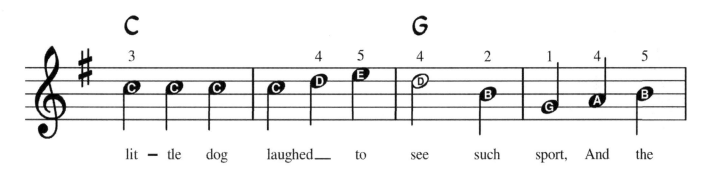

lit — tle dog laughed___ to see such sport, And the

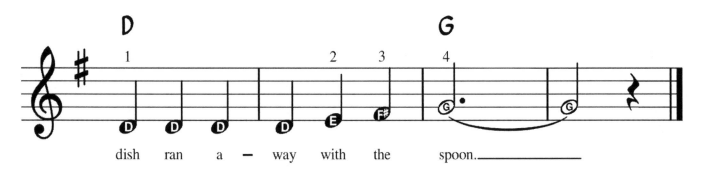

dish ran a — way with the spoon._____

Michael, Row the Boat Ashore

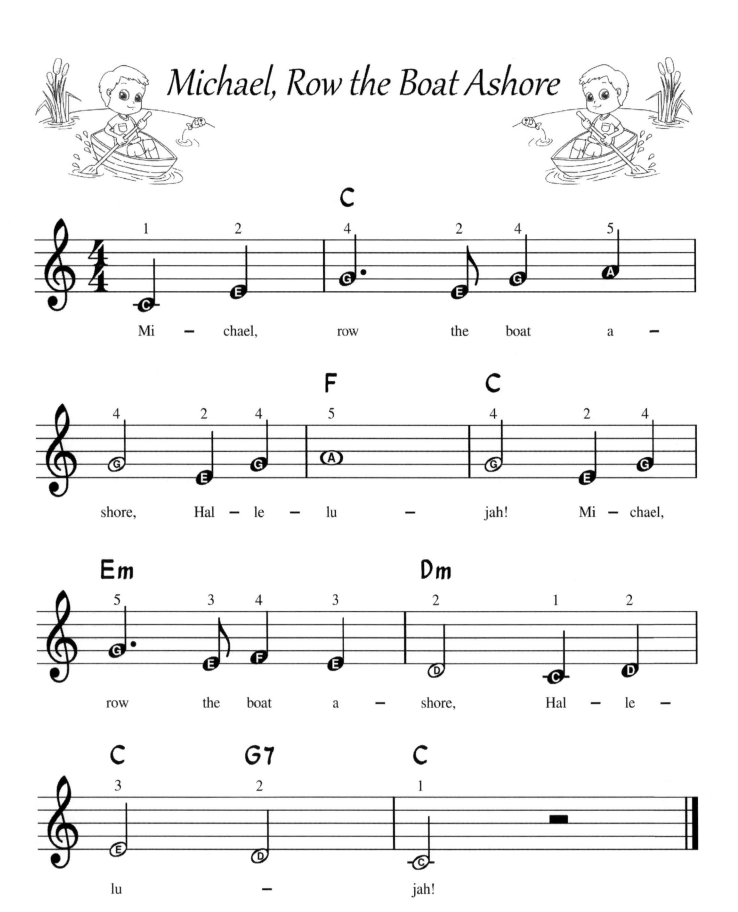

Comin' Round The Mountain

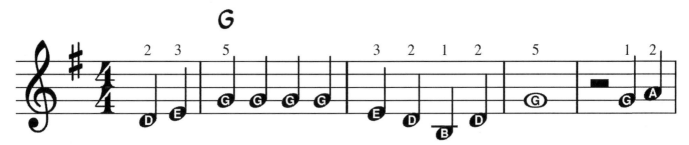

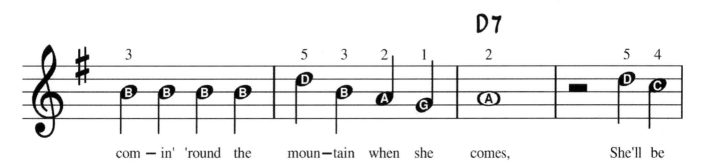

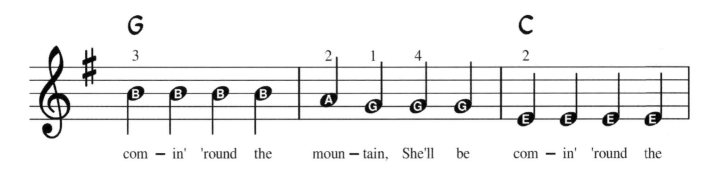

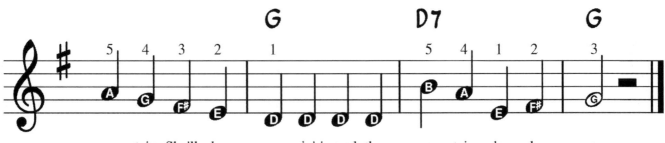

Polly Wolly Doodle

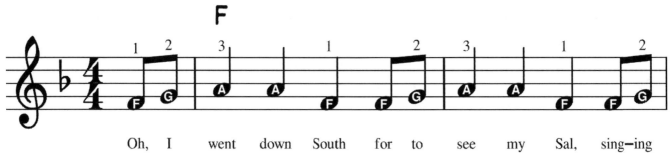

Oh, I went down South for to see my Sal, sing—ing

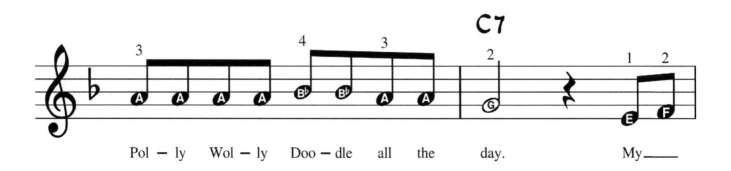

Pol — ly Wol — ly Doo — dle all the day. My____

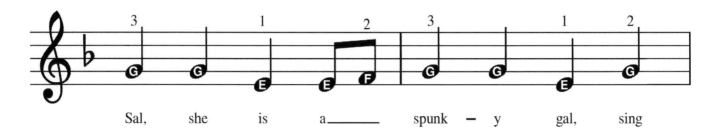

Sal, she is a____ spunk — y gal, sing

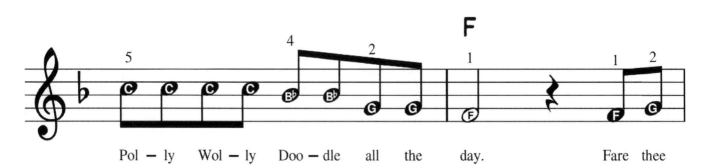

Pol — ly Wol — ly Doo — dle all the day. Fare thee

well,   fare   thee   well,   fare   thee

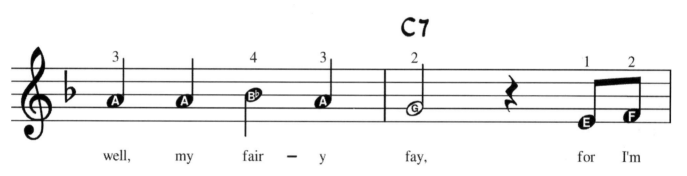

well,   my   fair — y   fay,   for   I'm

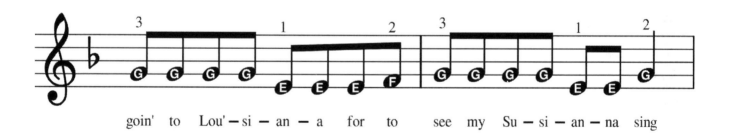

goin'   to   Lou'— si — an — a   for   to   see   my   Su — si — an — na   sing

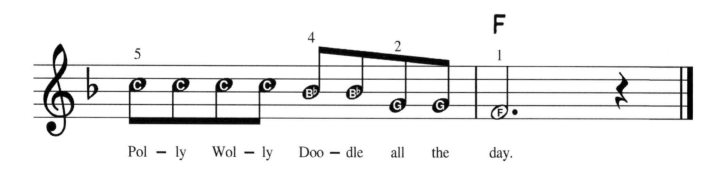

Pol — ly   Wol — ly   Doo — dle   all   the   day.

Bingo

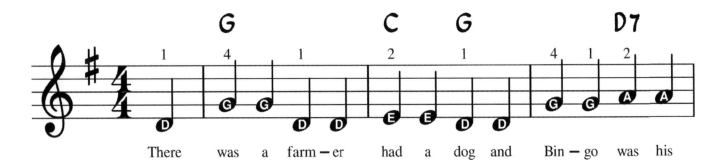

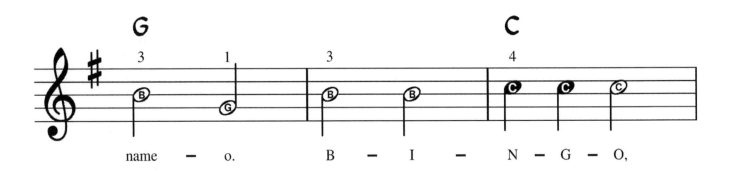

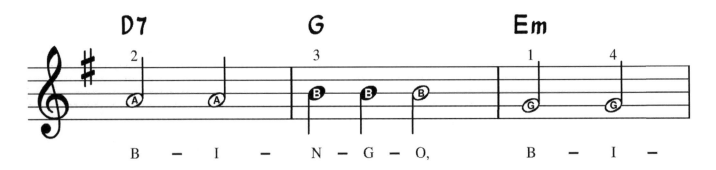

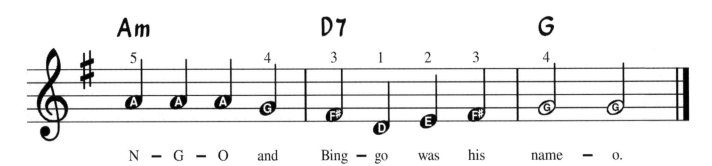

Sing A Song Of Sixpence

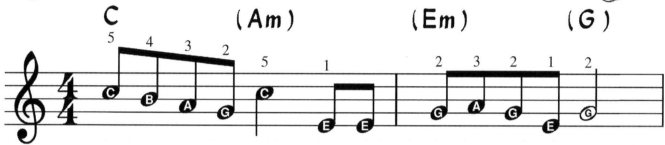

Sing a song of six — pence, a poc — ket full of rye;

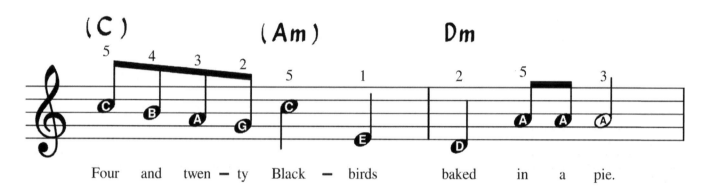

Four and twen — ty Black — birds baked in a pie.

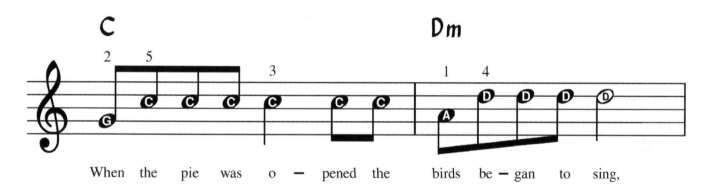

When the pie was o — pened the birds be — gan to sing,

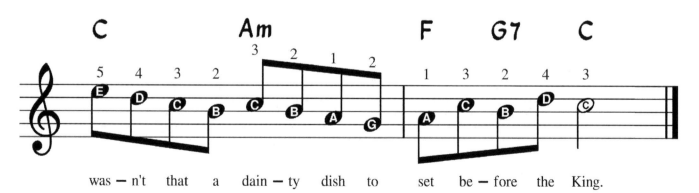

was — n't that a dain — ty dish to set be — fore the King.

We Wish You a Merry Christmas

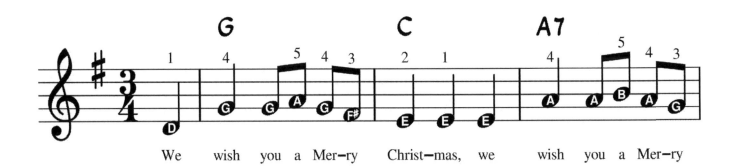

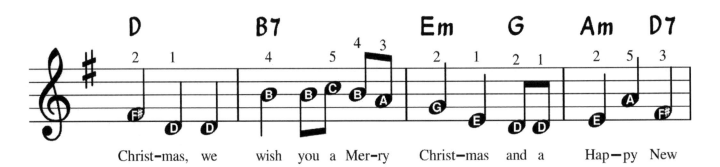

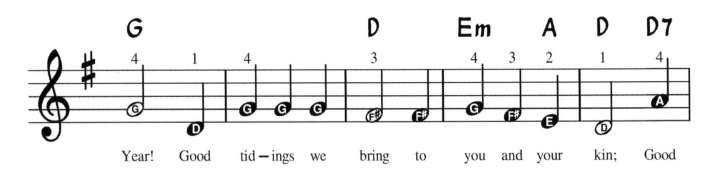

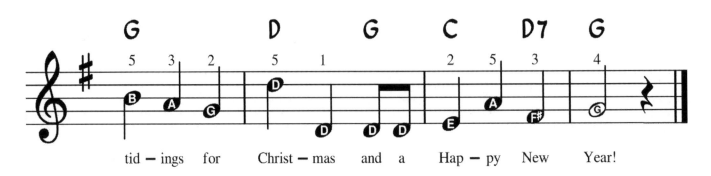

Minuet

By J. S. Bach

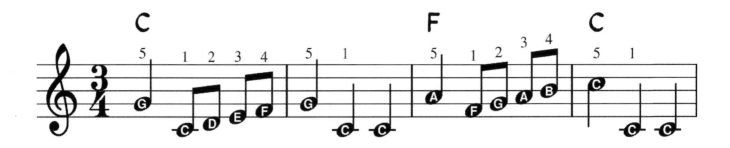

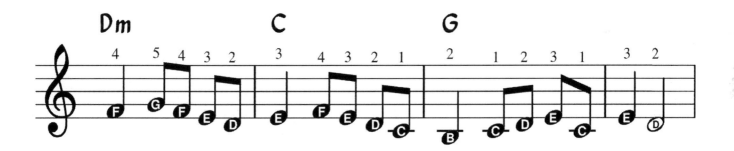

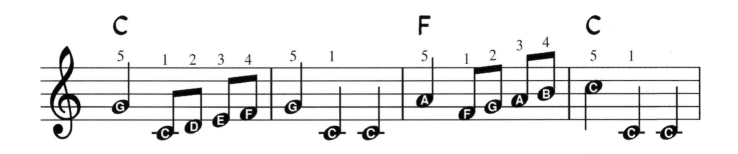

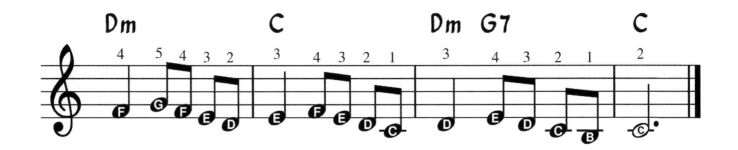

For He's a Jolly Good Fellow

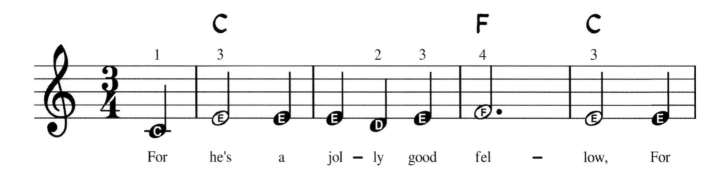

For he's a jol — ly good fel — low, For

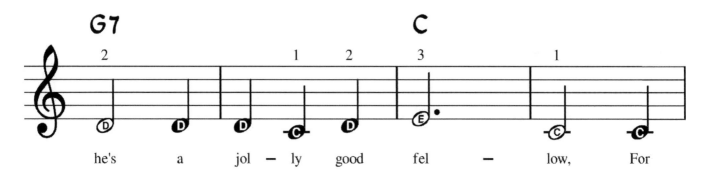

he's a jol — ly good fel — low, For

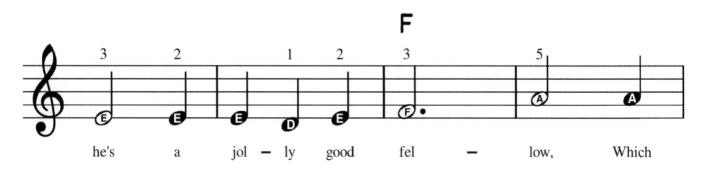

he's a jol — ly good fel — low, Which

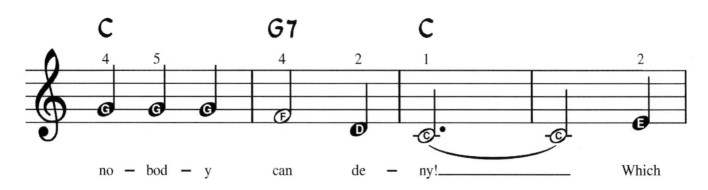

no — bod — y can de — ny!_____ Which

58

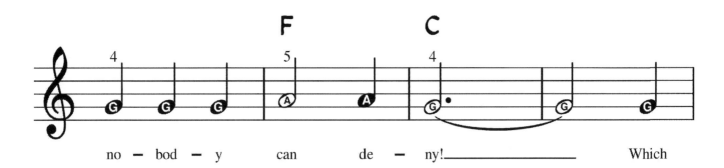

no — bod — y can de — ny!_____ Which

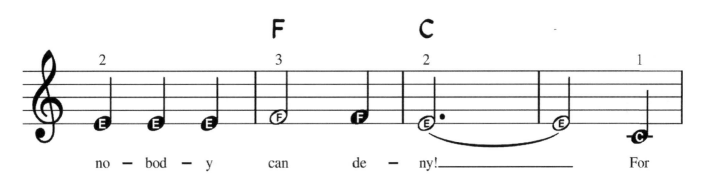

no — bod — y can de — ny!_____ For

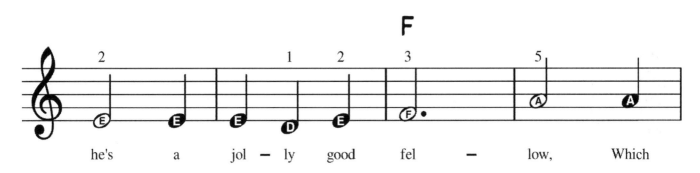

he's a jol — ly good fel — low, Which

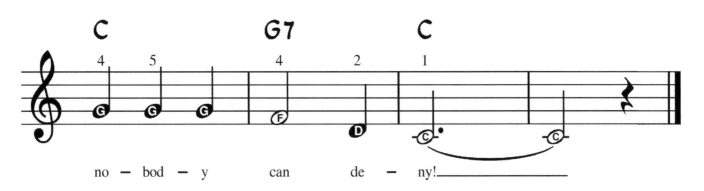

no — bod — y can de — ny!_____

The Mulberry Bush

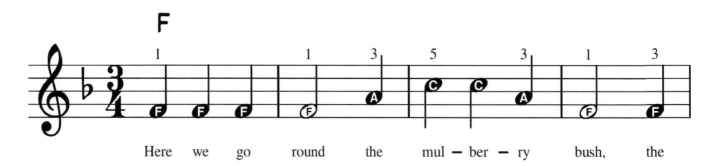

Here we go round the mul — ber — ry bush, the

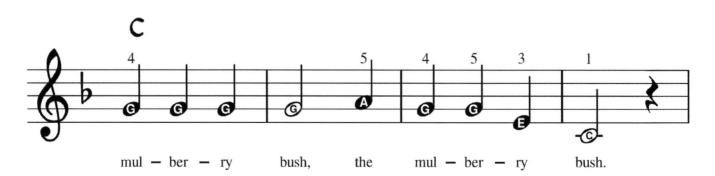

mul — ber — ry bush, the mul — ber — ry bush.

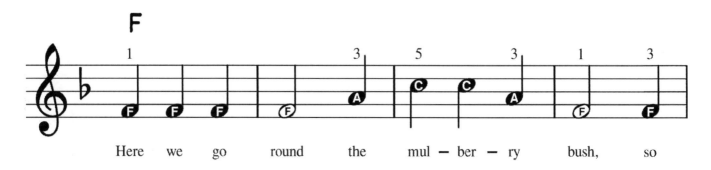

Here we go round the mul — ber — ry bush, so

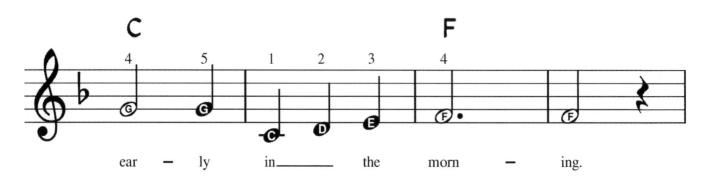

ear — ly in the morn — ing.

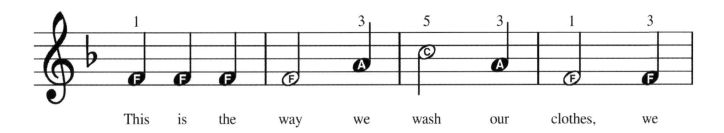

This is the way we wash our clothes, we

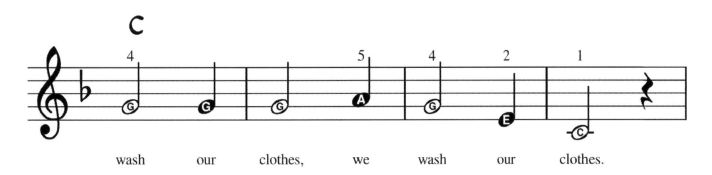

wash our clothes, we wash our clothes.

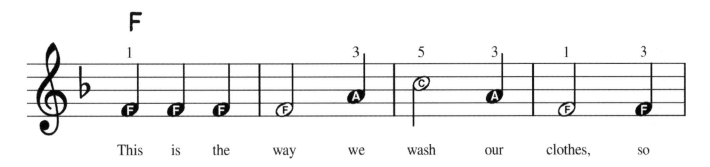

This is the way we wash our clothes, so

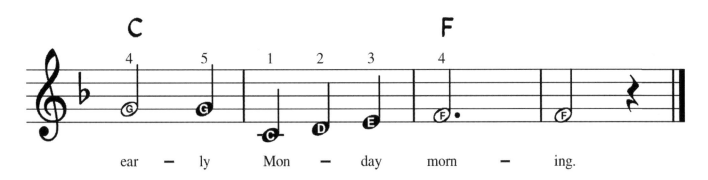

ear — ly Mon — day morn — ing.

Good King Wenceslas

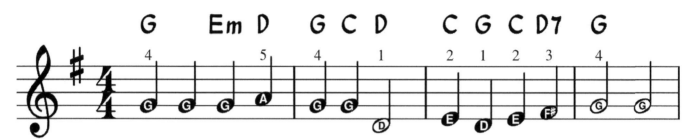

Good King Wen—ces — las looked out, On the feast of Ste—phen,

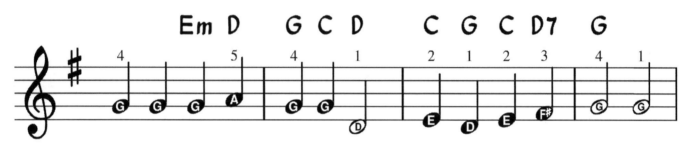

When the snow lay round a—bout, Deep and crisp and e — ven;

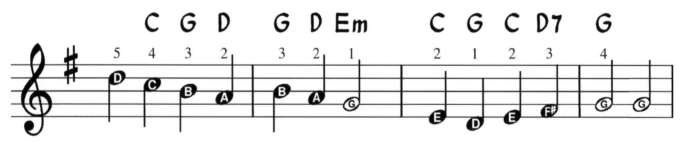

Bright—ly shone the moon that night, Though the frost was cru — el,

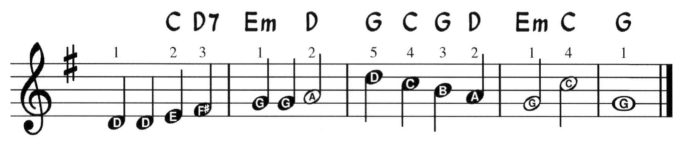

When a poor man came in sight, Gath—'ring win—ter fu — el.

Scotland The Brave

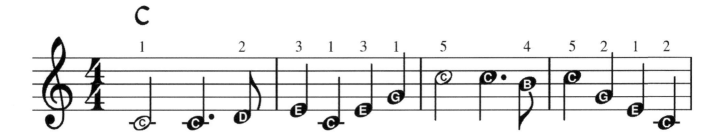

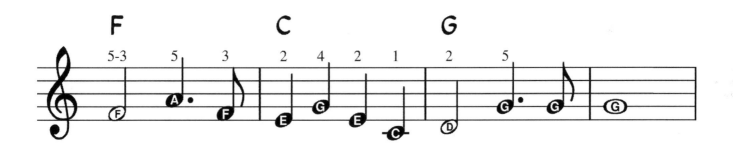

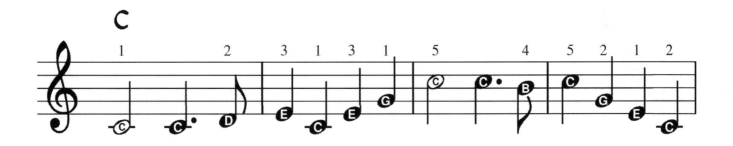

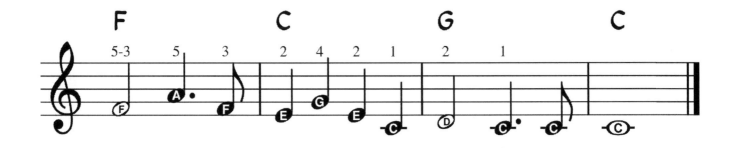

Home On The Range

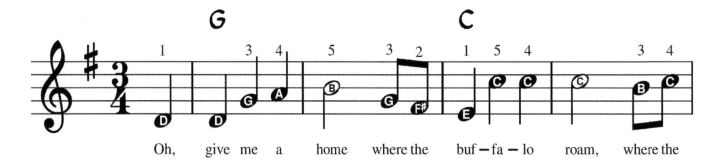

Oh, give me a home where the buf—fa—lo roam, where the

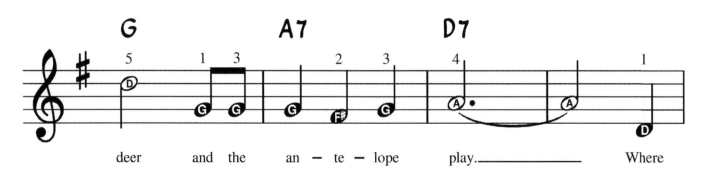

deer and the an—te—lope play._____ Where

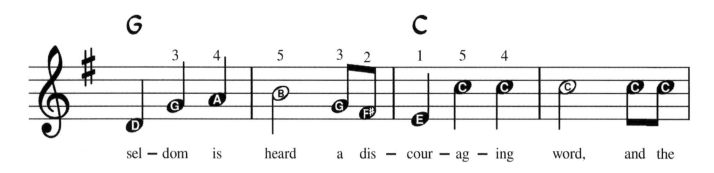

sel—dom is heard a dis—cour—ag—ing word, and the

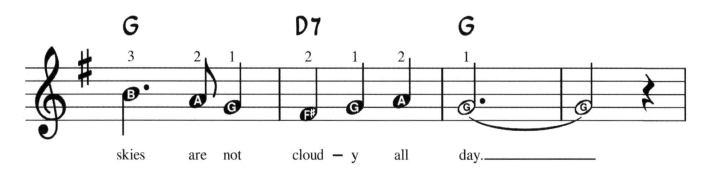

skies are not cloud—y all day._____

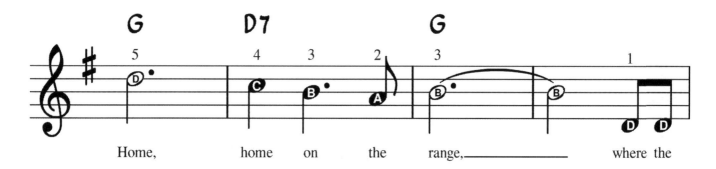

Home, home on the range,_____ where the

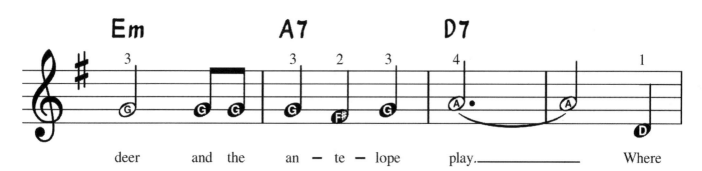

deer and the an — te — lope play._____ Where

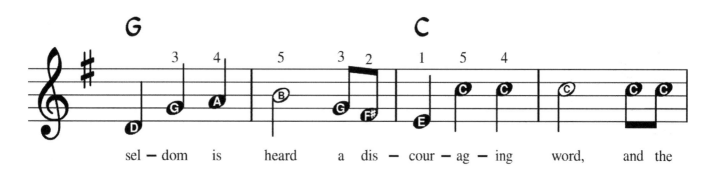

sel — dom is heard a dis — cour — ag — ing word, and the

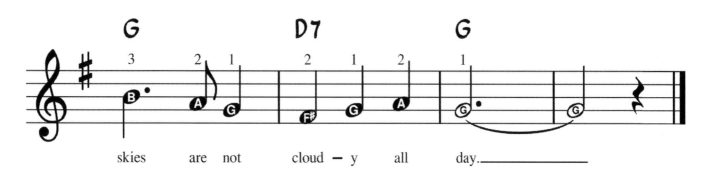

skies are not cloud — y all day._____

We Three Kings Of Orient Are

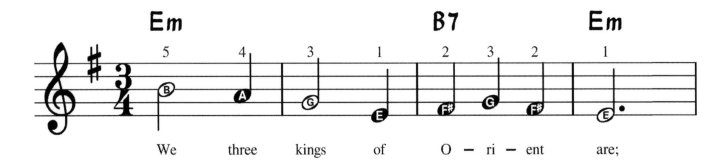

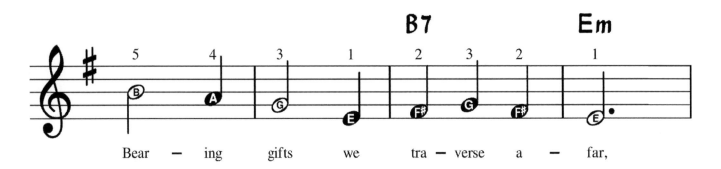

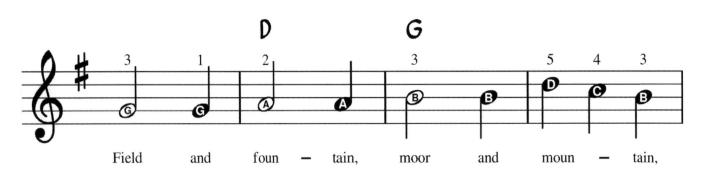

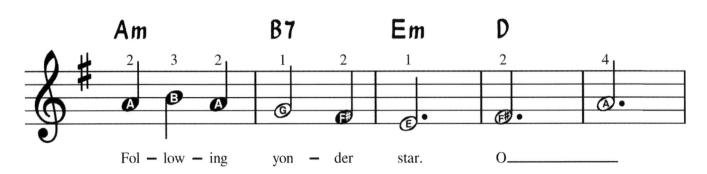

I Saw Three Ships

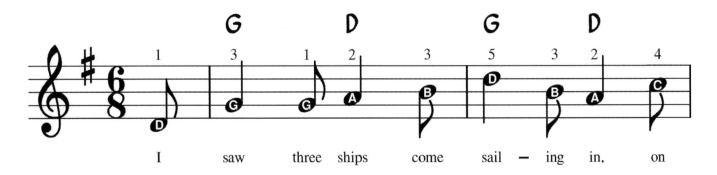

I saw three ships come sail — ing in, on

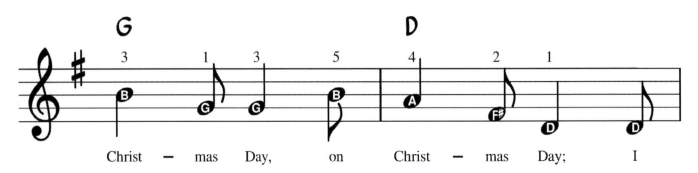

Christ — mas Day, on Christ — mas Day; I

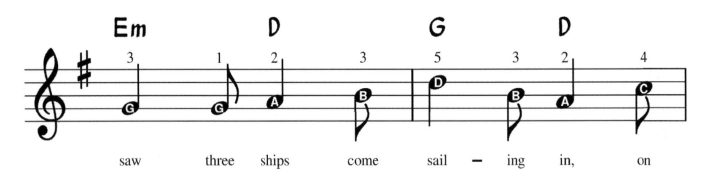

saw three ships come sail — ing in, on

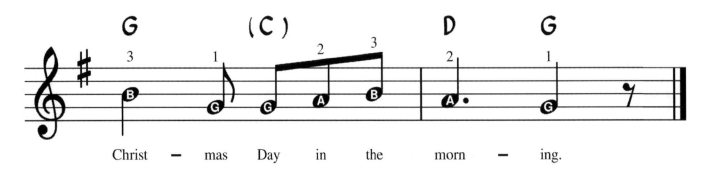

Christ — mas Day in the morn — ing.

Streets of Laredo

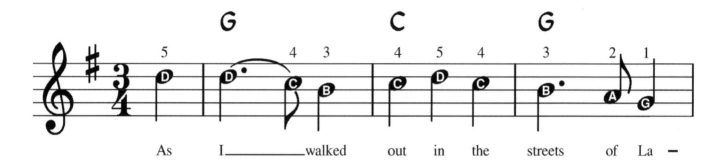

As I_____walked out in the streets of La —

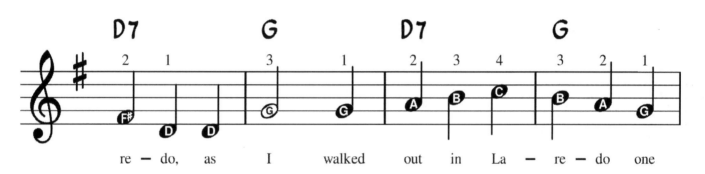

re — do, as I walked out in La — re — do one

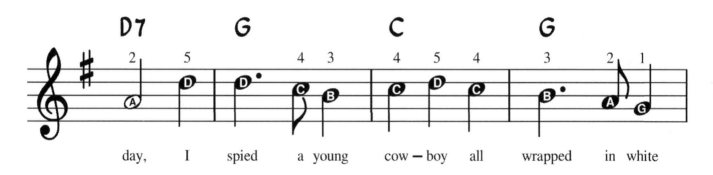

day, I spied a young cow — boy all wrapped in white

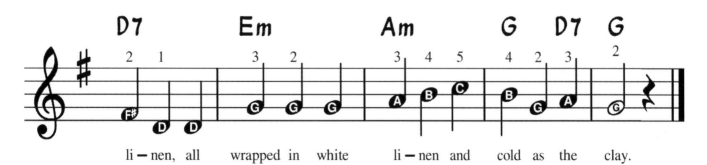

li — nen, all wrapped in white li — nen and cold as the clay.

Swing Low, Sweet Chariot

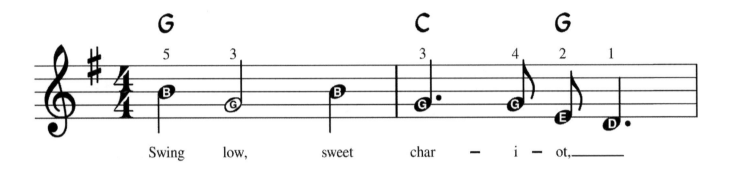

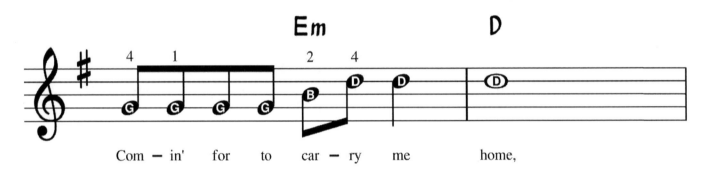

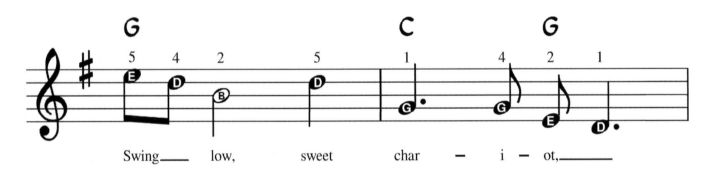

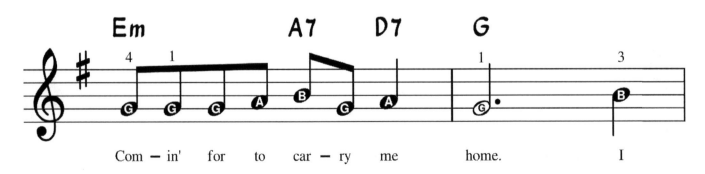

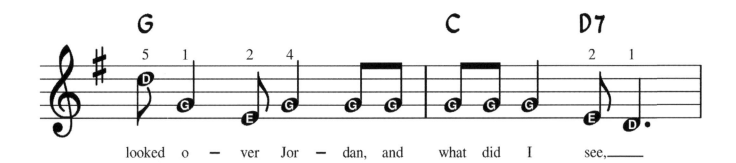

looked o — ver Jor — dan, and what did I see,____

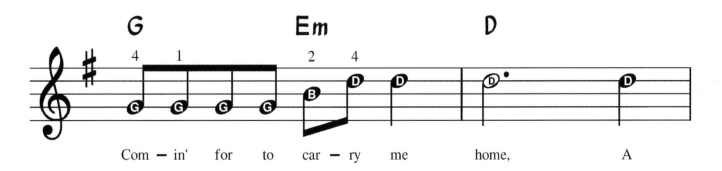

Com — in' for to car — ry me home, A

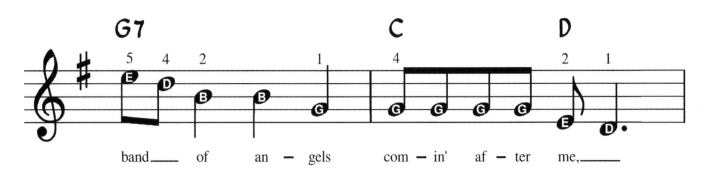

band____ of an — gels com — in' af — ter me,____

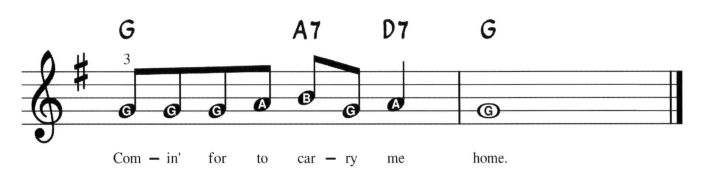

Com — in' for to car — ry me home.

Made in the USA
Middletown, DE
01 December 2020